The women's center

NO TURNING BACK: LESBIAN AND GAY LIBERATION FOR THE '80s

Foreword by
Malcolm Boyd

Gerre Goodman
George Lakey
Judy Lashof
Erika Thorne

New Society Publishers

Book design and layout by Nina Huizinga
Cover design by Julie Braxendell

ISBN: (Hardbound) 0-86571-019-8
(Paperbound) 0-86571-018-x

Printed in the United States.

New Society Publishers is a collective of Movement for a New Society,
a network of small groups working for fundamental social change
through nonviolent action.
This book has been reviewed by the North Country Regional Service
Collective of Movement for a New Society, acting as the representatives
of the MNS Network. It has our sponsorship as a valuable piece of
literature, with perspectives worthy of consideration and discussion.
The opinions stated herein do not necessarily represent agreed-upon
positions of either the North Country Regional Service Collective or
the MNS Network as a whole.

"I find NO TURNING BACK positive and heartening while bravely outlining the depressing and oppressive dynamics of patriarchy. What makes it positive in the face of this is its personable and visionary presentation. It acknowledges our oppressions without dwelling in anger. It gives us steps to take in order to move forward in our struggle, and it lets us know we're not alone."

—Peace Newsletter

"The book fills a long felt need for a progressive analysis and pragmatic sourcebook for lesbians, gays and others concerned with replacing patriarchal oppression with a more humane alternative. I was quite pleased by the integration of personal statements and experiences into the more theoretical discussion, and by the inclusion of practical and feasible proposals for individual and collective action. I look forward to using the book in my teaching ..."

—Larry Gross,
    Professor, Annenberg School of Communications,
    University of Pennsylvania
    and Co-Chair, Philadelphia Lesbian and
    Gay Task Force

"Not a public relations pitch for homosexuality, not a moralistic treatise on the importance of being nice to one another—NO TURNING BACK comes to terms with the hard realities of our experience and develops strategies to change them. All of the realities of homophobia and sexism that we like to deny or avoid dealing with are presented as places where real struggle can lead to productive change. This is the place where the lesbian/gay movement must be."

Harry Britt
Member of the Board of Supervisors
of the City and County
of San Francisco

Acknowledgements

We thank our dear friend Cynthia Mallory, who first edited *No Turning Back*, for her hard work, love and patience. She performed the difficult tasks of untangling endless sentences, clarifying impenetrable prose, and smoothing transitions from author to author.

We are equally grateful to Pam McAllister, who readied *No Turning Back* for publication, for her sensitivity, thoroughness and persistence. She polished and perfected the manuscript, eliminated jargon and tracked down missing footnotes. Pam responded to the demands of the weary authors and the anxious publishers with care and respect, and became a friend to us all.

Thanks also to Chip Coffman for typesetting, Stanley Marcus for copy editing, and Stewart J. Thomas for layout.

Finally, we must thank our comrades at New Society Publishers, David Albert, Matt Becker, Nina Huizinga and Paul Lieberman, for bringing this book to you. They worked hard and long to transform our manuscript into a book, consulting with us all along the way. We especially thank Matt Becker, NSP's liaison with us, for the flexibility, understanding and humor he displayed when we missed deadlines and cancelled meetings.

Permissions

"*Gay Spirit*" © Charlie Murphy, 1979, on the album *Catch the Fire*, from Good Fairy Productions, P. O. Box 12188, Broadway Station, Seattle WA 98102. For booking contact Steve Wells (206) 329-4863.

"*We Will Make the Changes*" © P. J. Hoffman 1967 (not on any album)

"*Don't Shut my Sister Out*" © Betsy Rose 1978, on the album *Sweet Sorcery* released by Origami Records, published by Origami Music.

Lyrics from "*Imagine My Surprise*" by Holly Near © 1979 Hereford Music, on the album *Imagine My Surpise* Redwood Records. All Rights Reserved. This album is available from Redwood Records, 476 West MacArthur Blvd., Oakland, CA 94609. Phone: (415) 428-9191 or write for a catalogue.

Lyrics from "*Can't Turn Back*" by Meg Christian © Meg Christian Thumbelina Music.

The poem "*The Weekend*" by S. C. is used by permission of the poet.

Contents

Introduction 1
  Liberation for everyone
  The new militancy
  The purpose of this book
  How this book came about
  To clarify our terms
Chapter I—How This Society Oppresses
Lesbians and Gay Men 9
  Lack of civil rights
  Secret or semi-secret lives for many gays
  Oppressive reactions to gayness
  Family
  The medical establishment
  Social change movements
  The heterosexual assumption
  Internalized oppression
  Conclusions
Chapter II—An Analysis of the System
of Gay Oppression 29
  Keeping women's energy from women
  Competitive masculinity
  Submission/dominance and sex roles
  The connection of heterosexism with other
    systems of oppression
  Class and classism
Chapter III—Breaking Free: A Vision of
Sexual Liberation 45
  What is sex for?
  Sensuality and sexuality
  Same-sex, opposite-sex
  Androgyny
  Institutions supporting androgyny and gay love
  The personal struggle

**Chapter IV—Five Stages of Struggle
for Gay Liberation** 55
Cultural preparation
Organization building
Confrontation
Mass noncooperation
Parallel institutions
In summary
Chapter V—Lesbian Culture and Strategy.........69
Lesbian culture
Lesbian relationships
The lesbian community
Urban lesbians
Rural lesbians
Lesbians of color
Class differences
Lesbian strength
**Separatism and Solidarity:
A Lesbian Feminist Perspective**
Separation changes the lives of individuals
Separatism helps build the women's movement
Bisexual women
Lesbian feminists and heterosexual women
Lesbian and heterosexual women
working together
Feminist and non-feminist women
Lesbian mothers with male children
Separation and men

Chapter VI—Gay Men: Culture and Strategy 95
Gay men's culture
Vitality of the gay world
Decadence
Getting it together:
   Problems in the gay men's culture
A feminist perspective for men
Effeminacy, or,
   Why are heterosexual men's wrists so stiff?
Relating to heterosexual and bisexual men
Married gays
Faggot fathers
A liberated movement for liberation
Chapter VII—We Can Make the Changes 121
Liberating sexuality
Next steps for non-gay women and men
Allies
Heterosexual women claim their own space
Next steps for lesbians and gay men
Unlearning the lies
Increasing our political awareness
Building alternative institutions
Campaigning for specific changes
Increasing our skills
Struggling against racism
Struggling against classism
Struggling against ageism
Struggling against chemical dependency
Struggling for adequate health care
Struggling against violence
Becoming powerful
Notes 145

Malcolm Boyd, social critic and author of 20 books, is writer-priest-in-residence at St. Augustine-by-the-Sea Episcopal Church in Santa Monica, California. He has described his gay consciousness and experience in two memoirs, *Take Off the Masks* (New York: Doubleday, 1978) and *Look Back in Joy: Celebration of Gay Lovers* (Gay Sunshine Press, 1981). He has taught gay and lesbian writers workshops at UCLA and USC under the auspices of the Gay and Lesbian Community Services Center of Los Angeles, and is a member of the Executive Committee of the Society for Senior Gay and Lesbian Citizens. Boston University has established the Malcolm Boyd Collection, a permanent archive of the priest/writer's letters and papers. He is a book reviewer for the *Los Angeles Times*, and contributes to a wide number of journals and newspapers throughout the U.S. He and his mate, John A. Due, live in Los Angeles.

FOREWORD

No Turning Back is a significant book. It places lesbian and gay liberation in the spiritual-social-political context of human liberation, thereby removing it from a shallow ghetto category. It recognizes essential similarities between situations in which lesbians and gay men presently find themselves, yet moves beyond this to a realistic appraisal of a studied, mutual and pragmatic separatism—this, for the sake of liberation at deeper levels. The book's authorship is a collective one, sophisticated, earnest, and resolutely seeking truth.

"Hard thinking, new research, practical organizing, experimental action, and strong personal support" will be needed, the authors tell us, to contend with "a new situation": an organized movement that uses "bigotry, plus sexism, racism, classism, and fear of all that's different, for its own political purposes."

To begin meeting a need for gay political theory that takes a comprehensive, holistic approach, the authors include "an analysis of oppression, a vision of liberation, and a strategy for change." They are inspired by Movement for a New Society (MNS), a national network of collectives founded in 1971 to work for radical social change.

Heterosexism is the term used in this book to describe the system which oppresses gays. "This society is fundamentally based on submission and dominance.... Gay people, gay relationships and gay liberation, threatening the ingrained dominance/submission roles, are profoundly subversive in the present society." Classism is linked to heterosexism; it "causes us to overlook the unique human qualities of a person and stereotype her or him according to one feature."

Five stages are postulated for the struggle for fundamental social change: cultural preparation, organization building, nonviolent direct action, mass political and economic noncooperation, and the transfer of power to new situations. It is suggested that gay activists "enthusiastically participate in coalitions for progressive change, while also developing the vitality of separate gay organizations."

Men can aid the feminist struggle by giving women support to be separate, and especially by learning to support and care for each other, the authors say. A side effect of women's separatism is seen as stimulating "major emotional growth for men."

Prophetically, the authors state: "the social changes we are proposing are for a movement in which the political is personal, the personal, political."

No Turning Back is a manifesto, a warning cry from the dark midnight of the soul, and a call to human liberation rooted in hope and love.

—Malcolm Boyd

Introduction

This book is for lesbians, gay men, and our allies.

We are facing a time of turbulence and difficulty. A well-organized move from the right is seeking to erase the civil rights gains of the past decade and hoping even to go further: to put gays back into the closet.

At first glance, the backlash is no surprise. When a group stands up for itself and demands change, there is nearly always another group which mobilizes to reassert the status quo. When Black people organized direct action for equality in the nineteen-sixties, the Ku Klux Klan and other racist organizations increased their activity. When women pushed for equality in the '70s, patriarchal forces stirred themselves to counter the threat.

If all lesbians and gay men had stayed discreetly in the closet, we could have avoided a fear-ridden reaction. We could also have continued to exist in our bars, in our fear and inhibited mutual support, in our absence of role models for young lesbians and gays, in our lack of a vibrant feminist culture. By censoring ourselves, we could have remained invisible.

Invisibility is an essential part of the oppression of gayness. Conservative leaders often tolerate homosexuality; after all, there are right-wing politicians, ministers, and celebrities who are homosexual. There is a tacit agreement among them not to be difficult with each other about that, as long as homosexuality stays in its place. What they cannot stand are visible lesbians, proud gays: those who "flaunt it."

The right wing agenda is more than a defense of the status quo. True, the right is appealing to that cultural conservatism which has never gotten used to the assertion of Blackness, of womanness, of Jewishness, of the other ingredients which were left out of the American Pie. But the right is using that cultural appeal to build a stronger political base for its own program, a program that includes an unprecedented military build-up, tax breaks for the rich and support of Third World dictatorships.

Lesbians, gay men, and our allies are therefore in a new situation. We are not simply dealing with bigotry that runs like a thread through so many of society's institutions. We also must now contend with an organized movement which uses that bigotry, plus sexism, racism, classism, and fear of all that's different, for its own political purposes. Confronting that is a deeper task. It requires hard thinking, new research, practical organizing, experimental action, and strong personal support.

We offer a framework for the strategies of the '80s and '90s. In it we show why lesbians and gay men standing up for ourselves are such a threat, why our issues are not seen as those of "just another interest group seeking its place in the sun." We offer a broad perspective which shows how gay oppression is linked to other forms of oppression in society, how the economic system is connected to the pain we experience, how everyone will benefit when gay liberation becomes a reality, how a strategy can be developed which protects civil rights while building toward liberation, how we can develop allies while still growing our new lesbian and gay cultures, and how we can nourish that strength in each of us which grows from our sense of self-worth.

Liberation for everyone

In a narrow and short-run way there are benefits provided by the system of gay oppression. Domination by non-gays of lesbians and gay men does not continue by accident; it performs functions for those with power. In Chapter II we will describe how those functions work. But gay oppression also hurts those to whom it gives privilege; when we look at the matter from a human point of view, even non-gays will gain from the liberation of lesbians and gay men.

A growing number of non-gays are aware of how constricted their lives have been by sex role definition. The culture offers two character ideals for everyone to aspire to, depending on gender. These character ideals include characteristics that complement each other:

Masculine	Feminine
logically rigorous	intuitive
cool, unfeeling	emotional
protective and tough	vulnerable
aggressive	passive
competitive	cooperative
productivity-oriented	nurturing
initiative-taking	responsive
violent, directly forceful	manipulative, indirect

and so on.

Human beings are not, of course, made so narrowly by nature, and these cultural straitjackets take a lot of getting used to. Some people never get used to the restraints, and much of the emphasis of both the women's and men's anti-sexist movements of the '70s has been to break out of these stereotypes. Non-gays as well as lesbians and gay men have worked at this.

What is often overlooked is that a force which gives these character ideals their power is *homophobia*—fear of, and contempt for, homosexuality.

In my high school anyone who deviated from a certain way of acting was called "queer." They didn't need to be gay, they only had to not fit in somehow. Students were called "dykes" and "faggots" pretty casually—it was just a way of controlling people. Except we controlled ourselves, really—by the time we were teenagers we already bought the system. *

When women are assertive and men nurture each other, they are immediately suspect, however heterosexual they are in fact. Homophobia, then, helps keep the masculine/feminine dichotomy in place, which deprives individuals of wholeness and maintains men's power over women.

In Chapter III we propose a way out of the sex role prison. Instead of the masculine/feminine dichotomy, we propose androgyny, which embraces the best characteristics now allocated to the two genders. We think each individual should be encouraged to develop her or his gentleness *and* assertiveness, initiative *and* responsiveness, intuition *and* analytic reasoning, exercising these characteristics as appropriate on her or his unique life journey.

The sooner we rid this society of heterosexism, the sooner androgyny will become an authentic possibility for everyone, whatever their sexual orientation. This is a vision which can unite us, for it implies liberation for everyone.

The new militancy

In the nineteenth century there was a wave of activity in Europe (with echoes in America) designed to promote homosexual rights and to explore the possibility of liberation [1]. That activity was interrupted in the twentieth century by the Second World War, where the strong German movement was especially subjected to the Nazi repression that resulted in tens of thousands of homosexuals being killed in concentration camps. [2]

In the U.S., homosexuals began organizing cautiously during the 1950s, but a society still intimidated by McCarthyism was not ready for an out-front movement.[3] The Black Civil Rights Movement expanded the tactics of dissent and made protest legitimate—at least legitimate enough so a mass anti-war movement could develop and activism could flourish in education, anti-poverty, and other areas.

The gay activist movement of today burst forth after the Stonewall riots of June, 1969, when gay men refused to submit in the traditionally intimidated way to a New York City police raid on a gay bar. Also at this time lesbians were active in the growing feminist movement. The liberal women's organizations attracted lesbians who felt the struggle for equal rights to be critical to their status as independent women. Radical lesbians

---

* Here and there throughout this book are thoughts and stories from our own lives and the lives of our friends. Such passages are delineated by horizontal lines, as here.

also took strong initiatives; less restricted than their non-gay sisters by ties to men, these women built feminist culture and militantly opposed the patriarchy. More and more of them came out of the closet, stating proudly that their feminism was connected to their lesbianism. In addition, many women involved with the feminist movement discovered in that context their ability to love other women.

From the eddies and currents of the '60s, lesbians and gay men brought many political perspectives to the new lesbian and gay movement: countercultural, personal growth, bourgeois reformist, Marxist, anarchist, pacifist, socialist, feminist, radical feminist, effeminist, and lesbian separatist. There was an explosion of gay activities: coffeehouses, consciousness-raising groups, demonstrations, concerts, dances, petitions, lobbying, publications, parades, and guerilla theater. Campuses sprouted gay student organizations. Gays both prominent and not well-known came out of the closet, often at considerable risk. All of these things are still happening; in some parts of the country activities have declined in frequency while in other places beginnings are only now being made. [4]

Gay caucuses now operate nationally among professionals, such as librarians, nurses, and teachers, and in movement organizations such as the National Organization for Women, the People's Party, and the Wages for Housework Campaign. There are many local gay organizations, such as Sisterspace in Philadelphia, Boston Gay Men's Center, New York Lesbian Feminist Liberation, Bay Area Gay Liberation; one reporter estimated 4000 autonomous lesbian and/or gay men's organizations in 1980. [5] The largest national organization is the Metropolitan Community Church; the largest gay civil rights organization is the National Gay Task Force. Recently a national radical feminist group—the National Lesbian Feminist Organization—and a gay socialist network—the Lavender Left— have been organized. There is, however, no nationally or regionally unified radical gay movement.

The purpose of this book

How can there be a united liberation movement for lesbians and gay men when there is little agreement on why we are oppressed, what a free society will look like, or how we can make change? In fact, there is no widely read or discussed proposal for gays which includes an analysis of oppression, a vision of liberation and a strategy for change. We share this book in order to begin meeting this need for gay political theory that takes a comprehensive, holistic approach.

In this we are inspired by Movement for a New Society (MNS), a national network of collectives founded in 1971 to work for radical social change. MNS joins personal growth and political work, welding the two together in the context of community. The organization combines open struggle through nonviolent direct action campaigns with grassroots organizing. MNS shares skills through training and alternative institutions, since revolution does not seem to be a quick or easy process. The MNS network is building a comprehensive world view that incorporates the large forces that create poverty, world hunger, sexism, racial discrimination, rape, mis-education, "queer-bashing," profiteering, the nuclear arms race, and so on. We offer this book as one building block for that comprehensive world view.

In this book we follow the MNS method of creating a multi-dimensional analysis, a picture of a life-centered society, and a way of making change. *Analysis* includes what is wrong now, and why. What are the roots of the problem? Where are the interconnections?

But analysis is not enough—it can leave us feeling overwhelmed and hopeless. So we wash the dust of today from our eyes sufficiently to see what might be tomorrow, and create a *vision*. Unity of vision is inspiring and gives us a stable reference point which can prevent reformism from corrupting our work—a danger now among gay civil rights activists who might settle for crumbs from the table of the privileged while allowing major forms of oppression to continue unchallenged.

A vision makes it easier to plan *strategy*. How do we get to our goals? How do we defeat heterosexism? The authors do not offer a complete, guaranteed strategy for gay liberation. Since such a revolution has never occurred, no one will know all the answers about building it until the process is well along, and even then we will know only what worked in that particular situation. Nonetheless, we share our extensive thinking on strategy for change, both general theory and organizational points, and specific next steps for different groups of people. We hope that others will continue to build on these ideas, forming a more and more effective strategy through trying, failing or succeeding, and constantly evaluating.

How this book came about

In May of 1975, Movement for a New Society commissioned a Gay Theory Work Group to write a working paper on theory and strategy for gay liberation. The paper, known as "Gay Oppression and Liberation," was finished in 1977 and circulated mainly among MNS members and parts of the lesbian and gay communities. Before the 1979 MNS National Network Meeting, a group of lesbians and gay men in Minneapolis/St. Paul organized the feedback and suggestions generated by the paper and made them available to a new editorial group which took on the task of writing this book.

The authors of the book are three lesbians and one gay man. Two of the authors of the paper, Judy Lashof and George Lakey, are still with the group; Erika Thorne and Gerre Goodman joined and saw this book through its ups and downs. We are aged 25-43, working class and middle class, white, and from different regions of the United States.

The book is the result of our life experiences and of nearly five years of research, theorizing, discussion, writing, and re-writing. We recognize that it is limited by the fact that we are white Americans. We hope that our book will be joined with the works of others to provide an analytical base for building a multiracial, worldwide gay and feminist movement. While it represents the opinions of the four authors, this book is also a working paper for Movement for a New Society and others to consider and debate.

The four authors of "Gay Oppression and Liberation" did not publish their names because one of them was unusually vulnerable to major reprisal. The other three did not feel comfortable taking credit for work that had been so much the collective product of all of them. MNS is working for the day when enough progress has been made so that our presently anonymous comrade can get the full and public acknowledgement that is deserved.

The book could not have been written without the emotional support and intellectual input of a number of people. So many have been involved at different points in this five-year process that we hesitate to name names because we would surely leave some people out. We must, however, express appreciation to our editors, Cynthia Mallory and Pam McAllister, who patiently labored with us and our various writing styles to bring about some coherence and unity.

To clarify our terms

Some of the most basic words are used by different people to mean different things, so we will define some terms immediately.

"Homosexual" describes same-sex love with an erotic dimension, or same-sex sexual activity. We do not use the term a lot because it has a clinical tone. We prefer "gay" and often use it in just the same way that "homosexual" would be used, which is the way "gay" was commonly used in the '50s and '60s in America. Since the advent of gay liberation, however, "gay" is often used to include a larger consciousness which includes pride and political activism. In this book, the context will usually show which meaning of "gay" we intend. Because of media distortions and male chauvinist realities in the often male-dominated gay rights movement, many women have been excluded by the term "gay." In this book we usually refer to "lesbians and gay men" to emphasize inclusion.

We use the term "non-gay" in this book to mean people who do not define themselves as homosexual—whether they call themselves heterosexuals, bisexuals, asexuals or identify themselves in some other way.

"Heterosexism," which is discussed at length in Chapter II, is, first, the suppression and denial of homosexuality with the assumption that everyone is or should be heterosexual and, second, a belief in the inherent superiority of the dominant-male/passive-female role pattern. Heterosexism results in compulsory heterosexuality which cripples the free expression and mutually supportive relationships of heterosexuals as well as of lesbians and gay men.

As we edited this book, it became clear to us that pronouns perform a very divisive function. They divide people into we and they, into you and us. We would have been happy politically to use "we" for all people— women and men, gay and straight, old and young—as an expression of our unity with all of humankind and especially with all oppressed peoples. This, however, would have been extremely confusing. We have therefore used the word "we" to refer to 1) the authors of this book, 2) all gay people (lesbians and gay men), and 3) humankind. Though all four authors take responsibility for the whole book, we've also used "we" in certain sections where it is much more immediate for lesbians (or all women) to speak directly (the chapter on Lesbians: Culture and Controversy, and the section on Keeping Women's Energy from Women); or for gay men (or all men) to do so (Gay Men: Culture and Controversy, and Competitive Masculinity). But when we refer to a particular part of the whole lesbian and gay population, such as older gays, Third World lesbians, bisexuals, or chemically dependent gays, we use "they." We hope it is obvious which meaning we are intending at which point, but we apologize for any confusion in the reader's mind.

We see this book as part of the ongoing process of liberation for gay people, both personally and politically. From the start, we've intended to present gayness as a positive, powerful force for change in American society, both in our vision of how things can be, and in our picture of current reality. We encourage you to send us your feedback, criticism, and additional thinking about our work.

Chapter I

How This Society Oppresses

Lesbians and Gay Men

What do we mean by "gay oppression"? Because we want non-gay readers to understand the reality of the way we have been treated, we attempt here the difficult task of describing this reality for those who have not experienced it. We want to be very specific, but at the same time convey the overall attitudes which are larger than the sum of single hurtful incidents. The reader already familiar with what gay oppression is like may wish to turn immediately to Chapter II, the analysis of how it works.

In this section we will look at the lack of civil rights for gays and the resulting secrecy, at the condemning reactions to gayness we encounter almost everywhere, at the heterosexual assumptions that pervade all of society, and at the destructive attitudes and behavior that have crept inside us as a result of our hurt. We will consider the way family and friends, the medical establishment and social change organizations relate to gay people.*

Lack of civil rights

Twenty-five states in the U.S. have laws which carry varying penalties for people who engage in "consensual sodomy." These laws apply to men and women, heterosexual and gay, but are used primarily to make homosexuality a criminal offense, even for two consenting adults in private. Most local ordinances and regulations across the country omit protective mention of gay/lesbian civil rights. This leaves room for prejudicial practices such as housing and job discrimination.

In the last decade many lesbians and gay men joined forces in the difficult struggle for legal reform. In a number of places gay rights legislation was

---

* Unfortunately, there has not been enough scientific study of the experience of lesbians and gay men, despite the large number of us (probably 13% of the population). Reliable statistics on how many gay men have been assaulted or lesbians have been denied employment do not exist. We are therefore forced to say "many" or "some" when we would like to be more precise, and look forward to the day when homophobia no longer inhibits studies of homosexuals.

passed, favorable judicial orders were issued, and executive orders were signed. A bubble of optimism began to form among gay activists and their allies. As usually happens, this progress encouraged a reactionary backlash (two steps forward, one step back!): the New Right took homophobic alarm and linked it with anti-feminist and anti-youth sentiment to create a crusade to "save the family." (The New Right coalition has also drawn on militarism, racist feeling, and hostility to unions in its effort to return to the "good old days" before the sixties.)[1]

The stirring up of anti-homosexual feeling succeeded in defeating some of the gay rights measures: in St. Paul, Minnesota, and Dade County, Florida, for example. In Seattle the anti-gay forces were beaten back through a coalition of gays, unions, and Black groups, but that was one of the exceptions.

Hope for change coupled with visible repressive backlash prodded lesbians and gay men to take increasingly open action on our own behalf. "Thank you, Anita" became a song popular among gay activists, referring to the singer and former Miss America, Anita Bryant, who, for a time, was the visible tip of a male-dominated anti-gay movement. Anita was thanked because the ranks of gay activists were swelled by the dramatic tug of war between forces for and against gay rights.

At this point the push for gay rights has become a mainstream political issue, but we are left with continued denial of civil rights for most lesbians and gay men, with legal gains in some places, and with a sober realization of how rigidly homophobic this society is.

Gays are specifically barred from many jobs, such as social work, teaching, the armed forces, and government jobs in many areas. Many of us must go to great lengths to preserve the secret of our sexual identity; the penalty for failure to do so is the loss of our jobs or the denial of the right to practice our professions: we lose our means of economic survival. Gays in nearly all jobs are liable to be fired if our employers find out we are gay, although an excuse other than our gayness is often given. Some gays put up with discrimination in promotion because we are "so glad to have a job at all."

Gay people rarely can buy property together, and it is often difficult to rent apartments together if we are "out" about our gayness. In big cities this often results in gay ghettos—areas where landlords charge more than the houses and apartments would ordinarily be worth and make large profits from gay people who want or need to live among supportive neighbors.

Gay people's relationships are not recognized as legitimate. Because there is no way we can claim gay family ties, we can be barred from visiting a sick or dying lover in the hospital, even if we have shared a lifelong relationship. We have no claim to a lover's property upon death, and no right to custody of the lover's children, no matter how long we have lived together. One vivid example is the treatment of Alice B. Toklas by Gertrude Stein's family. Ms. Toklas did not share in the author's estate and died a pauper.[2]

Laura was grieving over the death of Thelma, her partner of thirty-five years. At the same time she was faced with the stark reality of California's inequitable laws. She and Thelma were technically "unrelated," but Laura was the "widowed" survivor in joint tenancy; thus the law could extract three times as much inheritance tax from her as from a heterosexual widow. She was unable to prove (since they had kept joint accounts) that she had actually made half the payments on their house or that she had made 50 percent of the deposits to their checking and savings accounts. She was assessed 10 per cent of the total value of their mutual holdings—including even her half. Consequently Laura had to sell their home, which they had bought to "protect them in their old age," to raise the cash to meet the taxes.[3]

Mothers who are lesbians often lose their children; many courts have said that a woman who loves other women is not fit to love and care for her offspring. Some courts have permitted lesbians to keep their children so long as they abstain from gay relationships; thus a lesbian mother is forced to deny herself a lover or constantly fear discovery or appeal the courts' decisions and spend long years fighting agonizing and expensive custody cases.

Gay aliens must deny their homosexuality to be allowed into the U.S. In 1980, the work of the National Gay Task Force and others secured an end to probing interrogations into the sex lives of suspected homosexuals. Now the law reads: "Those individuals who self-identify themselves as homosexuals to Immigration personnel will be subject to exclusion."[4] A person wearing a button, T-shirt or other item which states that she or he is gay will be asked, "Are you a homosexual?" The answer, "No," will permit the person to enter the country without further inquiry.

With few exceptions, notably Harry Britt, member of the San Francisco Board of Supervisors, and Elaine Noble, former Massachusetts State Representative, lesbians and gay men are not represented on legislative bodies. Gay senators and congresspeople still feel compelled to remain in the closet and are unlikely to support a gay rights bill or take other action which might make their constituents suspect they are gay.

Secret or semi-secret lives for many gays

For almost all of us, there are real consequences to be suffered if our gayness is discovered. The possibility of legal sanctions is enough to keep some of us from expressing our homosexuality or sometimes even from admitting it to ourselves. Some of us try to "pass" or go straight and may be unfulfilled and unhappy.[5]

The urgent need not to be discovered keeps gays apart from each other. At work, for example, we are afraid to get together with other people who are or might be gay, because being seen together makes all of us much more suspect. This inhibits us from supporting each other on a one-to-one level, let alone speaking out collectively against the homophobia of our employers or fellow workers. Oftentimes gays feel a need to be actively hostile to each other—totally ignoring or being critical, unkind, or disapproving—so as to shield themselves from suspicion.

> Maybe there's another gay person or two in the office, but you hardly know each other; in fact, you avoid each other. If people saw you with him too much, they might suspect you were up to something. And you know as sure as hell, no gay sister or brother ever helped you get where you are. If anything the opposite is true. In fact how many of us know of an office with two gay executives who hate each other, two gay English professors in the department who are bitter rivals, the gay personnel director who avoids gay applicants like the plague. We all know that just to be on the safe side it's not a good idea to get involved with any gays on the job. Even the straights notice this, and they have an explanation right at hand. "Those queers are so neurotic they can't even stand each other."[6]

In many parts of the country, the only place where lesbians and gay men have been able to get together openly has been the bars. Gay bars are often owned by straight capitalists who tend to overcharge for food and drinks. Even in the bars, gays are not completely safe; there is always the fear of raids and reprisals by law enforcement officers, or of being recognized by someone who might report us to our employers.

Our preferred physical appearance may also give us away. Lesbians who prefer pants and workshirts to nylons and skirts face the choice of not being ourselves or of increasing the chances of discovery. The same is true for gay men who like to wear pretty clothes, beads or long hair.

All of us, gay and non-gay, live out our personalities through our bodies: mannerisms, ways of walking and standing, loudness. Women and men who dare to exhibit characteristics usually assigned to the opposite sex attract attention. Often such people are gay, because by definition gay people reject at least some of the sex-role stereotyping of our society. Again, for gays, the choice is between acting in a way which feels unnatural or running a greater risk of discovery.

Closeted lesbians and gay men have to endure humiliating talk about gays and gayness—jokes about "queers," vicious gossip about other people suspected of being gay, absurd generalizations and hurtful assumptions. It is very hard to listen to such conversation, yet many gays dare not interrupt it and must often even fake amusement for fear of raising suspicion.

It is not safe for gays to hold hands, cuddle, or show affection on the streets or in public places. Lesbians and gay men are not able to turn around and give that spontaneous kiss while going for a walk or rush up and give a lover a warm embrace when meeting at the airport. Lesbians have spent the night in jail just for kissing each other goodnight on a street corner, yet heterosexuals would not tolerate such restrictions on their relationships.

Lesbians who are on welfare or who are separated from their husbands but have custody of their children, have to fear government spies or private detectives paying snoopy visits at any time of day or night.

The need for secrecy makes it difficult to build and maintain good loving relationships. Secrecy vastly increases the complications and problems of being intimate, which is never a smooth and easy business for anyone! It adds insult to injury, then, when we have to listen to heterosexuals put us down for the frequency with which our relationships may be broken. (The closet also prevents many heterosexuals from knowing the lesbians and gay men who do sustain primary relationships over many years.)

Keeping our identity a secret is a strain. Living with constant fear is wearing, draining, and demoralizing. Being two different people in different situations produces a sense of "split personality," although the schizophrenia is external rather than in our heads.

Oppressive reactions to gayness

Reactions to gayness range from physical assault to a patronizing tolerance to aware acceptance. Knowing the range of oppressive reactions helps people gain the awareness that leads to acceptance.

Gays are assaulted, confined to jail, forced into psychiatric "treatment," and even murdered—all for simply being gay. "Queer-bashing" is a popular sport for some men; even if the police are there to observe the incident they may do little or nothing to protect us. Often the police find opportunities to treat us roughly.

City Hall, Philadelphia, December, 1975: Lesbians protesting in favor of gay rights legislation were beaten, kicked, and thrown down two flights of stairs by the Civil Disobedience Squad called in to evict them.[7]

Lesbians are the recipients of much violence simply because they are women. We share with all other women the dangers of sexual objectification, physical abuse by men who are larger and stronger than we, and rape. We also share the more indirect forms of violence, such as economic disadvantages, pressure to conform to a feminine stereotype in our jobs or families, and pornographic representation. It is not easy to separate which type of violence comes to lesbians because of our sexuality and which because of our sex, and there hasn't been much research on the subject. The Minneapolis Lesbian Feminist Organizing Committee did a survey in 1978 of violence experienced by lesbians in the Twin Cities. Of 44 incidents reported, 41 percent were physically violent and 59 percent were threatening in words or actions. In 24 percent, police or other officials were the abusers. 62 percent of the incidents were directly related to the respondents' lesbianism.

From this survey and personal experience, it seems that overt violence usually comes when we demonstrate, through actions or words, that we are lesbians. Most of the police-related incidents in the survey, for instance, happened outside lesbian bars. Most random violence was triggered by lesbians touching in public, becoming known in mixed company as lesbians, or not acting in "feminine" ways.

The threat of physical violence is one of the ways that women are kept from acting powerfully. Less direct forms of violence have the same effect.

Jo and I were sitting on two swings in a park at dusk, having a serious conversation, not touching. Suddenly we realized someone was deliberately shining a flashlight in our faces, and we saw a teen-aged boy on a bicycle. We yelled at him in the dark to get the hell out, but he just kept riding back and forth, snickering and saying, "Hey, girls, what are you doing?. . ." Jo took after him in rage, calling him names and threatening to bash his head in. I guess he'd never had women react to him quite that way, so he kept his distance, but followed us for blocks, bringing some friends in on it. "Hey, look at those lesbians!" "Nah, they're just friends. . ." "They're leh-heh-heh-hesbian friends." Finally he threw the flashlight at us and rode off. We were full of rage that we couldn't have an involved talk in the park like a heterosexual couple without this nerve-racking experience totally disrupting it.

Lesbian mothers are separated from their children. Lesbians stay in the closet for fear of losing their jobs. We are often completely disowned by our families or made to deny our identity when we're with them, never talking about our social lives, never bringing our lovers home to the warm welcome received by a son- or daughter-in-law. Many Third World lesbians are made to choose between their race and their sexuality—to be included in their culture in the traditional role of women, or to be more openly gay in the predominantly white visible lesbian culture—a gut-wrenching choice that produces years of hardship for many sisters. We are an invisible population, having to look harder for each other on all levels: a first role model for a strong, independent woman, a circle of friends, a lover, a job with others of our kind. These and many other forms of daily, indirect violence are a constant drain on our personal resources.

And then there is pornography: an extreme, degrading media reflection of the violence women experience in society. It exploits and degrades every aspect of women's sexuality, from childhood on, and furthers women's subjection by men. Lesbian love is portrayed in pornography as a teaser for men—the sexual preparation of women for the entrance of a man and the beginning of "real sex."

Gays, both women and men, are often ridiculed and called degrading, insulting names such as "queers" and "perverts." Even people who do not mean to be oppressive will often, on discovering we are gay, spill out all their feelings about gayness upon us—and, given society's attitude toward gays, such feelings are rarely positive.

Lesbians have to be prepared to deal with men who refuse to accept our own definition of our sexuality. Telling a man "I am a lesbian" is not an effective way to refuse a proposition for sex. On finding a woman is gay, à man is likely to apply even more sexual pressure rather than leave her alone. Instead of respecting her gayness, he may see it as an opportunity to make a special conquest that will prove his virility beyond doubt.

A common myth about gays is that we are sex-mad, that sex is much more central to our lives than it is to other people's. Gay men and women are always imagined in bed—not doing the laundry, dishes, cooking, cleaning, and paid work that are as much a part of our lives as they are of heterosexuals'. Gay men are often not permitted to work with children because it is suspected we will rape or molest them. This is nonsense: almost all child rapes are done by heterosexual men to little girls. In the same way, little girls are often considered to be unsafe with lesbians. This myth causes gay women special hardship, since so many of the jobs open to women are with children.

The emphasis on sex as the only important aspect of a relationship is patriarchal, and so is the definition of a gay person simply as someone who has sex with another of the same gender. We would like everyone to understand that gayness, on a personal level, has to do with love, commitment and energy as well as sex, and on a societal level, with breaking out of conditioned behavior and sex-role stereotyping. To reduce gayness to a simple question of sexuality is to belittle its impact both on the individual and on society.

A common experience for gays is having our friends leave us when they discover we are gay, often protesting at the same time that our gayness does not disturb them at all. Often it seems they are no longer excited about being with us; they sit on the other side of the room now and are afraid to touch us; they worry about their own reputations if they are seen with us too much.

On the other hand, some people want a "gay experience" but are not honest about the fact that they are only experimenting. Often we are abandoned after a sexual involvement in which an emotional commitment is made to a person who is not prepared to leave the safe boundaries of heterosexuality. Perhaps we thought we were helping the person come out, and forging a potentially serious relationship. Lesbians, for example, encounter activist feminist women seeking to expand their movement credentials by having a "gay experience" without being serious about their commitment.

Actually, it is remarkable how many people *are* able to accept our gayness, given society's strong negative conditioning. Often such people have reason to like us and trust us as human beings before they find out we are gay. When a gay person "comes out" to a friend, the occasion is sometimes much more significant and difficult for us than for the friend, for we are always afraid that our friends will withdraw from us when they find out we are gay.

We are angry when we are told not to be obsessed with our gayness by liberal heterosexual people for whom it is no big deal and who cannot understand why we keep bringing up the subject and "forcing it down their throats." It is hard not to be "obsessed" when our oppression as gays pervades every aspect of our lives.

The numerous myths about *why* gay people are gay are very painful to us, especially since they have such wide acceptance. Some myths are:

We were born unnatural, emotionally deformed, or hormonally unbalanced.

We are scared of people of the opposite sex or unable to maintain good relationships with them, perhaps because of previous bad experiences.

We are incorrigible man- or woman-haters.

We would really prefer to be the other sex and cannot accept or cope with our own gender.

We had strong mothers and weak fathers.

All of these myths look for *causes* of our gayness, thereby implying that it is abnormal and denying that our existence and way of life are usually natural and healthy. Very little research is done about why people turn out heterosexual because it is assumed that heterosexuality is the natural way to be. But widely held assumptions can be very wrong: a century ago in Victorian England it was assumed that women had no sexual feelings except for those few women who were abnormal. Misleading myths about homosexuality permeate all aspects of society but are reinforced especially by psychiatrists, novelists, and the media.

The most subtle reaction we encounter is that of patronizing tolerance, which on the face of it seems accepting of gayness but in fact indicates that heterosexuality is still much preferred. Such reactions are sometimes difficult to identify, but here are some examples:

Obviously avoiding any mention of our gayness.

Inviting a gay person to bring a "friend" to a social occasion, while everyone else is invited to bring his or her (heterosexual) "partner," "date," or "spouse" (i.e., not recognizing the equal validity of gay relationships).

Speaking positively of a gay person in a tone that implies that she or he is an exception, a good person *in spite of* being gay.

Family

Gay people must expect "oppressive reactions to our gayness" not only from strangers, acquaintances, and friends, but from our mothers, brothers, cousins, nieces. . . . We face a choice of trying to keep our sexual orientation secret from our families or of telling them about our gayness and hearing any of the following reactions:

"Oh, darling, whatever did we do wrong?"

"Of course I don't mind, dear, but I couldn't bear it if the neighbors knew."

"No, I don't think being gay is a sickness, but all the same I'd be glad to pay for you to see a good psychiatrist."

"But why don't you have an operation, dear?" (Yes, this really happened to one lesbian.)

"I have nothing against gayness, dear, but the only real fulfillment in life is having a (read: heterosexual) family and children."

"I just want you to be happy, dear, and it's such an unhappy life."

"Why can't you just go out and relate to men/women normally like anyone else; there's nothing wrong with you."

"You are never to bring any of your gay friends into my house." (particularly oppressive for young gays still living with parents.)

"Get out of my house and never come back; you're not my child any more."

Any of these responses is more probable than acceptance.

Gays who decide not to deal with such reactions, or who know in advance that coming out can only worsen our relationship with our parents, also face a tough time. We must be prepared to tell lies to people we love and to have ready (false) answers to questions about what we've been doing, where we've been, with whom, why, and what our future plans are. Then, in painful irony, we can expect to be accused of being silent and reserved, and of not sharing ourselves and our lives with our families.

Gay people are sometimes deluded into thinking that it is only the secrecy that is causing us problems with our parents, and that if we "came out" the relationship would be fine. Of course this is not true: gays have the same family relationship problems as non-gays.

But if we don't come out to our parents, it puts extra distance between us because there are so many details of our lives we cannot tell them. It can be particularly painful not to be able to share the happiness and excitement of a new or good relationship or not to be able to ask them for support during rough times with our lovers or when a relationship is breaking up.

"Coming out" to our children can be traumatic, too. We must be prepared to deal with all kinds of homophobic attitudes that they have absorbed or been taught. Because of the need for secrecy, many lesbians must ask our children, who are often quite young, to keep our intimate relationships secret from their fathers (our ex-husbands). It is painful to us to have to put such a burden on the children we love.

The medical establishment

Families, schools, the welfare system, the legal system, religious institutions and other mainstream structures all reflect and maintain the anti-gay orientation of society. The medical system is a major source of difficulty for lesbians and gay men.

Psychiatry is the worst offender. Many psychiatrists, by searching for "causes" of gayness and then inventing "cures," reinforce the myth that homosexuals are sick and deviant. (Actually, there are psychological studies which show gays to have personalities which are, on the average, at least as well, and perhaps better, integrated and more flexible than those of non-gays.[8]) Since people usually go to psychiatrists because they are unhappy or troubled, psychiatrists usually see only those gays who feel upset and not those who feel healthy, happy and self-confident. And although psychiatrists don't conclude that all heterosexuals are unhappy because they see only unhappy heterosexual clients, they do tend to assume that all gays are unhappy because their gay clients are.

The "cures" that psychiatrists devise are often extremely painful in themselves; for example, electric shock treatment and aversion therapy. Further, the mere concept of a "cure" for homosexuality is oppressive. The legitimacy of psychiatry is used to make people think gayness is a problem. Because many of us have been socialized into believing this, psychiatrists can make a good profit from homosexuals who come for treatment.

Changes are coming slowly. In 1973 the American Psychiatric Association voted, despite great opposition, to remove *homosexuality* from their list of "sexual deviations" and to substitute in its place a new phrase, *sexual orientation disturbance.* This was meant to apply to gay men and lesbians who are "disturbed by, in conflict with, or wish to change their sexual orientation." In the late '70s this was again changed to a new diagnosis, *ego-dystonic homosexuality,* supposedly referring only to those gays whose homosexual arousal is a persistent source of distress. This big change, then, amounts to little more than a more subtly expressed negative view of homosexuality.

> *This new category of psychosexual disorder is restricted to homosexuals; by definition it does not apply to heterosexuals who find their sex lives with members of the opposite sex a source of persistent concern and wish them to be different. Diagnosticians examine individuals dissatisfied with heterosexuality with a view toward improving their functioning as heterosexuals...*
> *The fact that "ego-dystonic heterosexuality" is not a diagnosis reflects a continuing implicit belief that homosexuality is abnormal.[9]*

Relationship counseling for gay couples is almost nonexistent, despite the wide range of therapies and social work establishments available. Lesbians and gay men have problems and conflicts in relationships like everyone else, but instead of getting responsible counseling we may be told to try changing our sexual orientation.

Medical doctors usually share psychiatrists' assumptions about gayness. Since they deal mainly with the physical rather than the emotional, their homophobia has fewer opportunities to damage us. However, most medical doctors lack information about specifically gay problems.

One lesbian had a vaginal infection and was told to abstain from sex while it was being treated. She asked: "Do you mean from intercourse or do you mean from oral sex or do you mean from touching?" The doctor did not know the answer. The medical profession assumes that sex equals heterosexual intercourse.[10]

There are special difficulties around venereal disease or birth control. Doctors rarely think to check, or to ask if they should check, for VD symptoms in the throats or anuses of male homosexuals. If asked to examine these places, they often make offensive remarks. Some doctors insist on giving pregnancy tests to all women suffering from disorders of the "reproductive system" (note the heterosexual assumption as to what that part of a woman is for), even if they can say with certainty, as lesbians can, that they are not pregnant, and furthermore, that they do not need any kind of birth control.

In order to get all the health care we need, gays must come out to our doctors; then we must face all of their negative attitudes toward gayness. Even this does not ensure good care. Many doctors, once they know we are gay, tend to blame all pains and disorders, physical and emotional, on homosexuality, even when it is totally unrelated to the medical problem.

When one of us expressed emotional or physical pain not even related to her sexuality, the medical doctor or psychologist told her, "It's all because you're a lesbian." The road to health is always seen as becoming heterosexual.... Our problems are not human problems; they are made into lesbian problems which would go away if we became heterosexual.[11]

Jody: "I had pelvic endometriosis, a noncontagious disease that women can get from a bad abortion or low progesterone production." Her male gynecologist hassled her with questions about how she made love and why she was gay, then finally said, "I strongly recommend that you see a psychiatrist. You're clearly very emotionally upset because you're a lesbian, and I think it would help you to deal with your disease if you began to work out your feelings about men."[12]

Moreover, it is risky to come out to our doctors, because they may then record our gayness in our permanent medical records, to which most medical establishments, not to mention various government agencies, have access. Thus we may be damned if we *don't* come out to our doctors, and probably damned if we do.

Social change movements

Activists have been subjected to homophobic conditioning just like everyone else, and unless they have actively worked to rid themselves of they are likely to have the same reactions to gayness as more conservative folks and to carry into their social change work oppressive attitudes toward gays. Despite varying degrees of homophobia, however, and always at some cost to ourselves, gay people have been active and important in almost every movement for social change. It is time that non-gay activists recognized both the important work that gays have done and the pain we have had to suffer within these movements for "liberation" as well as in society at large.

A gay man was active in the peace movement in the 1960s. He had a love relationship with another man, who was also an activist, which had lasted twelve years. People were beginning to suspect them of homosexuality. To preserve the respectability and acceptability of the peace movement, these two men moved into separate apartments. Their relationship broke up as a result.

Gays within social change movements face some special hurts as well as the more general negative reactions to gayness. When we bring up issues and concerns about gayness, it's painful to have non-gays accuse us of being divisive. Instead of recognizing that we are voicing an awareness of a division that we live with all the time, many radicals perpetuate that division by telling us that gayness is not the main nor even an important revolutionary issue and that we are diverting everyone from the basic struggle. Gay liberation is often trivialized, both in theory and in practice, by radicals who have never taken the trouble to analyze gay oppression carefully nor to read gay literature and find out what gay liberation is really about. Some Communist Parties have even gone so far as to condemn homosexuality as "an ideology of the petty bourgeosie" and to refuse to allow membership to known gays. However, this stance is now being fought by gay Marxists, using Marxist theory itself to show the revolutionary importance of gay liberation.[13]

Non-gay radicals who do have an understanding of gay liberation tend to be very vocal in their opinions about how gays should run our struggle for liberation. Of course gays welcome careful thinking and feedback; but one of the dynamics of oppression is the assumption that the oppressed are stupid, inferior, and unable to think for themselves. Non-gays should avoid telling gays how to organize.

Gays within social change movements are often asked to keep quiet about our identity and the struggle for lesbian and gay liberation so as not to offend people the movement would like to reach who might be deterred by militant, or simply open, gayness. A lesbian panelist at the East Coast Lavender Left Conference near Philadelphia in 1980 told the audience that the Marxist group of which she was a member excused her from its socials because it would be "awkward" for her to bring her lover. This is a denial of the importance and legitimacy of gay struggle; gays must not be pushed back into the closet so as to accomplish more "effective" outreach for the movement as a whole.

The heterosexual assumption

The continued assumption that everyone is and ought to be heterosexual, despite evidence to the contrary, is as widespread as it is offensive. Homosexuals live in an alien world, surrounded by novels, movies, television, popular music, advertisements, and sex manuals that refer exclusively to heterosexuality. This huge silence about the life of gays confirms our non-identity in society's eyes. Worse, many gays internalize this attitude. As Jill Johnston says in *Lesbian Nation*: "Identity is what you can say you are according to what they say you can be."[14]

Homosexuality is rarely an option that is presented to us. Thus, it is a major struggle merely to define, let alone feel comfortable with, an identity and way of life which should naturally give us joy. The lack of recognition by our culture is one of the reasons why we need to keep on publicly affirming our existence.

The total silence about gays by educators is particularly distressing and harmful. Never a word about homosexuality is said in most schools. When the human body is studied, biology teachers speak only of heterosexual sex and reproduction. Sex education deals with heterosexuality alone and assumes, erroneously, that intercourse is the only natural and satisfying sexual activity. Accurate information about female sexuality, which indicates that autosexuality (creating one's sexual pleasure oneself) and homosexuality are at least as satisfying as heterosexuality, is withheld, if the teachers themselves ever learned it! Historians omit mentioning, fail to discover, or deny that many famous women and men are now thought to have been gay; for example, Paul Revere, Queen Christina of Sweden, and King James I of England. Most literature teachers do not tell their students that certain authors were (or probably were) gay or bisexual, even when their gayness was important to their writings: Walt Whitman, Lorraine Hansberry, Mark Twain, Emily Dickinson, and others.

Gay artists throughout history have been absorbed by the dominant culture and their gayness concealed, or else rejected and unknown. Either way, gay history/herstory and culture are denied, and we are kept from gaining a real sense of ourselves and our place in the world.

Gay people quickly encounter the power of the nuclear family in our society. The (heterosexual) family is the basic unit of social organization in the West; and there is tremendous pressure for everyone to conform to it. The extent of this pressure is rarely understood until a person has tried openly and totally to reject it and thus discovered how often and how strongly we are told that success lies in getting married and having children. Gay people by definition opt out of this structure, and as a result they suffer much rejection and ostracism. Married people who discover they are gay are caught in a painful dilemma.

Lesbians have a particularly hard time with the heterosexual assumption. Not only are we daring to break out of women's traditional role of wife and mother, but we have to deal with sexual propositions and passes, people who try to arrange (heterosexual) dates for us, and questions about marriage. Often a lesbian is not free to confront these situations honestly, for fear of losing a job (especially if the propositioner is the boss) or friends, or, in the case of a hitchhiker, for fear of making the man even more sexually abusive.

I finally worked out a way of dealing with the hitchhiking situation that does not increase the risk of my being sexually assaulted, yet takes the opportunity to do some consciousness-raising about gayness. When the subject of sex comes up, I hedge; but when I get out and am safely on the sidewalk, I say, "By the way, the reason I am not interested in having sex with you is that I am a lesbian. Goodbye."

The religious establishments of this country reinforce the heterosexual assumption by recognizing only heterosexual relationships and by explicitly condemning homosexuality. For Jews and Christians, the Bible appears to state unequivocally, when literally interpreted, that homosexuality is a sin: "You shall not lie with a male as a woman: it is an abomination" (Leviticus 18:22); and, "Neither the immoral nor...homosexuals will inherit the kingdom of God" (1 Corinthians 6:9-10). Thus homophobia is sanctified and perpetuated by religious teachings.

Moreover, the religious institutions support the nuclear, heterosexual family as the only acceptable way of living (other than celibacy), condemning homosexuality indirectly but just as completely as in an outright statement. Though there are few pro-nuclear-family statements found in the New Testament (in fact Jesus said "Leave your family and follow me"), the position statements issued by United States churches endorse the family to the exclusion of other lifestyles. For example, a statement by the American Baptist Churches proclaims that the family is ordained by God as a primary institution. Even those churches which support gay rights consider homosexuality a deviation from the norm and do not support gayness as a valid way of life, despite their acceptance of known homosexuals into their churches. The United Presbyterian Church has said that laws which make a felony of homosexual acts privately committed by consenting adults are morally insupportable and contribute nothing to the public welfare. But it has added that such laws inhibit rather than permit changes in behavior by homosexual persons. That addition makes its real bias clear. (Happily, there is currently a tremendous amount of creative furor being generated by gay men and lesbians who are attempting to turn the churches around, and gay churches as alternative institutions are becoming important within the community.)

Society tends to discount many of our early gay relationships and feelings for people of the same sex (such as "crushes" on teachers and older students). Those experiences are considered not important, to be grown out of, or, at best, practice for "the real thing." Worse, gays come to believe these negative attitudes and values and tend to see the important, early relationships as being heterosexual ones, even when the reality is the opposite.

It is only now, as I review my past with a gay consciousness, that I can claim it as mine and recognize my gay feelings and actions as gay. It is especially important for me to reclaim my lesbian past, because I never recognized it as such at the time. Such is the way that our herstory is denied us; we don't even recognize some of our own personal experiences until years later, if at all.

Heterosexual assumptions about sex are particularly pervasive. Most people assume without thinking that there will be no sexual activity if the sexes sleep apart. This often works to our advantage in practice (as when we take a same-sex "friend" to our parents' home and are allowed or encouraged to share the same bedroom) but the assumption is oppressive. Homosexual sex is put down by being described as "mutual masturbation" instead of recognized as a valid way of making love and communicating affection. Even the physical definition of virginity is heterosexual and cannot be applied to homosexual sex.

Open displays of heterosexual affection are considered legitimate, while public homosexual affection is taboo.

I remember feeling panicky when a gay lover was particularly affectionate with me in the living room of my largely heterosexual communal household. Only later did I realize that the same activity by heterosexuals was warmly approved by everyone in that house, including me.

Those who tolerate homosexuality but view it as weird or abnormal instead of fully understanding and appreciating it are being condescending. And liberals who are comfortable leaving gays to "do their own thing" sexually but are afraid of the possibility that there may be a gay side to themselves are still assuming that heterosexuality is superior or absolute.

This heterosexual assumption has restricted and distorted all of us and all of our relationships, non-gays as well as gays, and its punishment and oppression have hurt and continue to hurt gays every day of our lives.

Internalized Oppression

We not only have to deal with a homophobic society; we must also struggle with our own conditioning—all the anti-gay feelings, beliefs, attitudes and behaviors that we have been taught and that we have unconsciously adopted as our own. As young people we were told that gays are to be avoided and gayness hidden because homosexuals are perverted, unhealthy, unhappy, disgusting, and likely to molest heterosexuals. Sometimes it was said directly through queer jokes, verbal attacks, and threats or reports of violence. Others of us heard more subtle comments:

"How unfortunate Uncle John is like that."

"She's such a nice person, too bad she's not normal."

"Boys can't kiss boys."

"Don't worry that you sometimes have sexual feelings for other girls; it doesn't mean you're a lesbian."

Like all children, we had a strong sense of justice and love and respect for all people. It hurt us to see anyone viewed or treated unjustly. But bit by bit we began to accept what we were told. We absorbed anti-gay beliefs before we knew that we were gay. It was often only with great difficulty that we could acknowledge our own gayness, for then these beliefs would apply to us.

Thus, like all oppressed groups, gays have come to believe on a deep level society's message that we are weird and inferior. This lack of self-respect, self-love and self-confidence is a major factor in keeping gays from standing up for our rights. If we do not feel good about ourselves, we will lack the strength and motivation to fight for liberation, and we will most likely despise and dislike other gays, since we've been taught that gays are not worth loving and respecting.

Many gays are convinced that gay is sick, and that it is healthier to be heterosexual. Wishing we were not gay and trying to find a way to change, we look for what is wrong with us. It does not occur to us that we may be healthy and society may be sick. As a result, many gays go into therapy. Although the gay liberation movement has caused some therapists to view homosexuality as a healthy option, too often gays are further confused by therapists who reinforce the belief that homosexuality is a sickness or, at best, an "arrested stage of development."

Those of us who think gayness may be a sickness often find ourselves loath to talk with non-gays about previous sexual experiences, knowing that they often look for that "bad experience" that "made us gay." Afraid of anti-gay attitudes in others because we half believe they may be true, we may find ourselves isolated from any support.

Many of us tell people we are gay fearfully and in embarrassment, as though admitting there is something wrong with us or to be ashamed of, even if consciously we do not believe that. If a person laughs at a gay button we are wearing, we tend to laugh too, as if it were a joke, something to be dismissed and not recognized as serious and important. Gays are sometimes defensive and apologetic about being gay, looking for approval and acceptance from other people and "hoping they won't mind," instead of being assertive that gay is good and that many people have a gay side that they should be in touch with.

A lesbian moved into a communal house and timidly asked if the other people living there minded that she was gay, instead of asking brightly how many other lesbians there were in the house.

Some gays fall in love mainly with non-gay people, feeling affection which they cannot express or which rarely has a chance of developing into a meaningful relationship. The gay person may have an inner contempt for gayness which leads to dislike of other gays and the belief that non-gays are "better." This cuts off the possibility of reciprocal relationships. The gay person may also be attracted to non-gays out of a sense of self-hatred, unconsciously setting up punishment for being gay by putting him or herself in frustrating, if not hopeless, situations.

We may feel guilty when we are attracted to non-gay people, as though it is all right to feel such feelings only for other gays. Even those of us who do not think it evil to be attracted to heterosexuals may feel we have no right to let them know how we feel, on the rationalization that it is not legitimate/fair/kind for us to encourage people to recognize their potential to be gay. Some of us are afraid we will "corrupt" friends and relatives by our gayness and do not think it is good to be influencing people close to us by a gay perspective. Again, the underlying (il)logic is that it is preferable to be heterosexual.

Gay people may even feel this about our lovers: that they would be better off heterosexual. This can lead to guilt that our relationship is merely prolonging our lover's "affliction." If these feelings are strong enough, we may give up the relationship or push our lover to become involved in a heterosexual relationship, at the expense of our own happiness. This is what happens to Stephen, the heroine of the classic lesbian novel by Radcliffe Hall, *The Well of Loneliness*. Stephen has loved Mary very deeply for a long time, but she pretends to be lovers with another woman to force Mary to leave her for a male friend, Martin. She explains:

> I can't give her protection or happiness [because I'm a woman], and yet she won't leave me. There's only one way....[15]

Unfortunately this is not just a literary device but an accurate reflection of the feelings of some gays. The self-destructive power of such guilt should not be underestimated. As gay people, we are often so relieved when we find that a friend is willing to talk about our gayness that we will listen to any kind of nonsense s/he says, even when it is a putdown of gayness. We may do this partly from a low sense of self-worth, which can lead us to feel, "I'm grateful for whatever small crumbs I can get, and probably I don't deserve even those"—instead of being positive about our gayness and demanding the kind of support we really deserve. Similarly, we are often so glad for any kind of friendship from non-gays that we may not notice when it is patronizing, or, if we do, it doesn't occur to us that we deserve something better. This self-invalidation also leads some gays into bootlicking behavior at work: doing more than our share of the dirty work for the boss because we are so grateful for "being treated as human beings."

Some gays internalize the myth that "heterosexual is better" by trying to emulate heterosexual relationships, and thus become trapped into stereotypes (e.g., being "butch" or "femme"), confining ourselves to an unreal role instead of being our natural selves. Of course, the lack of alternative models also contributes to role-playing.

Our feelings of low self-esteem, coupled with the conviction that there is not much we can do to change things, often make us feel basically powerless. Drinking or using drugs helps us to forget our negative feelings, relaxes us and gives us a false sense of being in charge of our own lives. As a result there is a high incidence in our communities of drug and alcohol abuse.

Since we are dependent on capitalist society to supply us with alcohol, or on the illegal market to supply us with other drugs, the problem is compounded: we must go to those who oppress us for chemicals to blind us temporarily to our oppression.

Drugs make it easier for patriarchy to control us as well, because people who are strung out on drugs or alcohol, even if only on weekends, will have a harder time thinking clearly about their situation. A chemically dependent person, whether a working-class man drinking beer on weekends with the boys, a housewife who takes tranquilizers for tension, an unemployed person on heroin, or a gay man taking amyl nitrate at a bar on Saturday night, will be less of a threat to the established order.

Gays who become chemically dependent are often further confused when, upon seeking "help," they are told that their gayness is the reason for their substance abuse problem. Because those staffing most drug and alcohol programs in this country have accepted the concept that alcoholism and drug addiction are illnesses, and because they cannot or will not see the political implications of drug and alcohol use, they are in a very weak position when it comes to offering the kind of support such a person needs to begin to feel strong and to give up these substances. Instead, the addiction, like so many other things (unemployment, violence against women, slums) is made the fault of the oppressed.

Clearly, the way gay people are socialized to believe the myths about ourselves is as destructive to our emotional health as it is effective in helping to maintain the system of heterosexism. Gay people have to root out systematically most or all of these inner attitudes from our belief systems—a long and painful task—before we have a chance of becoming comfortable with our gay identities; that is, with *ourselves*. Many never make it. But it is crucial that we repair these rust spots of self-contempt because they are so debilitating to ourselves and our struggle to be whole people. Self-respect is essential for emotional health and the struggle for our rights.

Rust spots, however, cannot simply be painted over; first they must be sanded clean. In order to accept the new paint of gay pride, we need to read and see and hear positive, accurate portrayals of gay people. We need to talk with other gay people. We need to recount the lies we have learned and how we have been hurt and proclaim loudly that we are gay. We need safe places to release the feelings of anger, frustration, grief, and fear which this talking brings up.

Conclusions

Heterosexism is very deep and widespread, affecting every aspect of gay people's lives. The result is that it is impossible for us to be ourselves and to act as we wish to, even when we have finally sorted out who we are. The process of discovering our gay identity is a mammoth and painful task because of the almost unbroken silence about homosexuality and the abuse that we usually get when the silence is broken.

Gay people are repeatedly faced with a dilemma—to come out and risk experiencing the pain of being rejected or stereotyped, or to stay in the closet and thus be essentially dishonest about who we are. This is not a choice that can be made once and then forgotten; it has to be made in every new situation in which we find ourselves, with every new person.

Chapter II

An Analysis of the System of

Gay Oppression

The way gays are treated and the pain we suffer are part of a fabric of oppression in our whole society. Despite gay community centers, educational programs and civil rights laws, ignorance and hatred of gay people and attacks on us will continue until the institutions that benefit from this oppression are removed.

Just as the oppression of Blacks is the result of a racist society, the oppression of gays is the result of a heterosexist society. The term "gay oppression" is often used to refer only to the fact that some people are looked down upon and discriminated against because of our sexual preference. The term "heterosexism," on the other hand, refers to the *cause* of the oppression—the socialization of all people to fear their own and each other's homosexuality, and the reinforcement of traditional dominant male/passive female social/sexual relationships. Heterosexism makes an institution out of heterosexuality and enforces it through ideology and social structure. It shapes all of society and harms all human relationships by so narrowly and rigidly restricting the range of our experience and expression of affection.

A complex, self-contained system of oppression, heterosexism is also a form of sexism, a part of patriarchy. It maintains the subservience of women to men by punishing homosexuality and any deviance from the currently accepted range of masculine and feminine heterosexual roles.

Some heterosexuals are upset by the term "heterosexism" because they feel it blames all of gay oppression on what they do in bed. On the contrary, heterosexism pervades all of society, not just bedrooms. Although, like sexism and racism, the system was not created by heterosexuals living today, most of today's heterosexuals do identify with it, perpetuate it, and cause gay people pain by their prejudice against and ignorance/denial of homosexuals and homosexuality. For example, heterosexual couples may take for granted being able to kiss goodbye at train stations or walk arm-in-arm through a park without realizing that these common expressions of affection are privileges in this society because they are denied to same-sex lovers.

All men and women working for change must learn to separate their heterosexual practice and their identities from the oppressive *ideology* of heterosexism, which must be opposed. To do so, they need to question their own orientation and the assumptions about relationships that go with it. It is only early and persistent conditioning that keeps many people from exploring the homosexual side of themselves, and unless heterosexuals work themselves free of such conditioning, they can't help but collude with the oppression of gays and gayness. Thus we continue to use the term "heterosexism" to describe the system which oppresses gays.

Since heterosexism is part of patriarchy, its essential features are different for women and men. We begin this section with an examination of how heterosexism keeps women's energy from women. We then look at how it is used to force men to participate in competitive masculinity. We view and explore further the relationships between heterosexism, sex roles, and the structure of submission/dominance. We make connections between heterosexism and other forms of oppression. And finally, we discuss the class system and its effects upon gays.

Keeping women's energy from women

Heterosexism prohibits sexual relationships between women and, in so doing, helps to keep us* from forming any intimate connections with our own sex. Fear of an emerging sexual element has destroyed many women's friendships.

Recently I met a young lesbian couple who had been best friends throughout high school—until they made love. One of them could not bear the reality of a lesbian relationship, so, although desperately needing each other's support, they vowed not to see each other again. Many women keep this vow, avoid further close friendships with women, and rush into marriage. Fortunately my friends, after a month of separation and severe depression, made love again. They have been lovers ever since.

If not destroyed by inner fear, a lesbian relationship may be interrupted by outside authorities such as teachers, parents, husbands, employers, counselors. In *Rubyfruit Jungle*, Rita Mae Brown describes the consequences of the discovery that Molly (modeled after herself) and her roommate, Faye, are lovers. The students in their dorm tell the college authorities, who expel the two and notify their parents. The following is a passage from the letter Faye leaves when her father takes her home:

God, Molly, they're all crazy. My own parents want to lock me up. Mother was crying and said she'd get the best doctors there were for her little girl and what did she do wrong. Vomit! I think we won't see each other. They'll keep me away and you're locked up in the hospital. I feel like I'm underwater. I'd

* In this subsection "we," "us," and "our" refer to women.

*run away by myself but I can't seem to move and sounds run in and out of
my head like waves. I think I won't surface until I see you . . . . Molly get
out of here. Get out and don't try to find me. There's no time for us now.
Everything is stacked against us.* [1]

The homophobia (fear of homosexuality) of their dormmates, the college
authorities, and Faye's parents succeeds in destroying the couple's
friendship and Molly's college career (she is on scholarship).

But homophobia can also be very subtle. Irene Schram, author of the
essay "Woman Becoming," explains that she developed a pattern of making
close temporary friendships with women without realizing that whenever
a relationship became intense, fear of her own homosexual potential caused
her to end it.[2] These are just a few examples out of thousands. Any lesbian
and many women who are not "out" can relate how homophobia has
damaged a friendship for them.

Prohibiting sex between women also works to prevent us from making
a total commitment to each other. Women are taught that marriage—or
a "primary" relationship—is the only basis for an ongoing commitment
to another person, and of course this relationship must be with a man.
Clearly, sex is not a prerequisite for committing oneself to someone, but
the myth that it is increases the pressure for women not to make
commitments to each other. Often the fear of the possibility of
(homosexual) sex is enough to keep two women from making such a
commitment, even to an explicitly non-sexual relationship.

In deciding where to live or go to school, a woman will often plan to
live with or near her boyfriend or (male) lover. Yet she will not think of
changing her plans to remain with a woman friend. If a woman's husband
decides to leave town for a new job, she will not consider staying behind
to be with a woman, even if she is closer to her than to her husband.

A sexual relationship with a man will call forth a commitment to spend
time with him frequently, to work through problems, and to think about
"the relationship."

I've been friends with several heterosexual women, with whom I
would have liked to have had a "relationship." Even though they
assured me that they liked me, I did not become the priority to any
of their lives that a male, whom they enjoyed in the same ways but
who was a potential sexual partner, would have become.

The above quote illustrates how a woman can be trapped by two equally
oppressive myths: one, women cannot have sex with women; two, sex is
necessary for commitment. These myths work together to define women
in terms of men.

Heterosexism, as we have said, transforms heterosexuality into a coercive
institution. Lesbianism is repressed in order that women not commit
ourselves to women, in order that we be available to serve men. We are
separated from one another to prevent us from overthrowing patriarchy.

Not only does heterosexism prevent or punish homosexuality, it promotes and rewards heterosexuality. Girls are told that happiness lies in finding the right man. They are beseiged with advertisements in newspapers, magazines, radio, and television for clothes, makeup, toothpaste, and deodorants to help them make the catch. Movies, novels, television shows, and magazines all focus on the importance of attracting Mr. Right. Relatives and friends always inquire about dates, boyfriends, and ask, "When are you going to get married?"

Marriage is rewarded by numerous economic advantages. Wedding presents help to furnish a home. Discounts for wives or spouses are offered by airlines, travel agencies and resorts. Social security, employee health plans, and recreation programs expand to include the spouse. One justification for lower wages for women is that they will be supported by their husbands.

Marriage provides status. A woman is entitled to the privileges of her husband's social class. A married woman is seen as dependable, moral and trustworthy. Marriage is often the only way that partners of different nationalities can reside in each other's countries.

Heterosexism also controls women's relationship to sex per se. Most women learn how we should function sexually from our experiences with men and from books and movie scripts written and produced by men. Men are concerned with what feels good for them, or with having a woman who performs in the ways they are taught to desire. Women are told by men how other women *respond* sexually; we are discouraged from exploring together how we *function* sexually, or what sort of sexual activity we like. The prohibition of sex between women keeps us from experiencing our sexuality with someone who has the same questions, the same responses, the same genitals.

Discovering and exploring our sexual selves with other women could be a natural, healthy and positive experience, both for learning about sex and for creating women's energy. Instead, because of heterosexism and in spite of the so-called sexual liberation of women, women learn that sex is for the pleasure of men. This means that a) women do not know the joys of sex with women, and b) women are willing to accept whatever sexual behavior a man desires, including falsifying our own sexuality, faking orgasm, and then trying to appear satisfied.

While learning not to love other women physically a woman learns not to love herself physically by looking at herself, touching herself, or masturbating. The physical and spiritual connection between loving herself and loving another woman is well expressed by Irene Schram in "Woman Becoming":

I am a woman writing a song to a woman. The woman is myself. The woman is another woman. I'm no song writer but I am writing. I'm not so sure I'm talking about myself, or women loving women . . . the lines blur. With great beauty though, like undulating lines of sun on waves, in the middle of the ocean, halfway between one continent and the next, the lines of definition barely existing, at least always moving, never holding still between being a woman loving yourself and being a woman loving women. Same breasts, same warm skin. Same softness, and particularly female sense of life and joy, such laughter and nurturing possible.[3]

To completely love ourselves, it may not be necessary to love other women. However, the conditioning that we are weak, incomplete—needing a man for strength, fulfillment, and protection—tells us that we cannot love women, even ourselves, that we must serve men; it also tells us to include ourselves under a category meaning inferior and not worthy of commitment. Loving another woman, because it contradicts this conditioning, inevitably leads to greater self-love.

Competitive masculinity

Whereas women are separated from each other to prevent them from overthrowing patriarchy and defining and directing their own lives, men within each economic class work together in such a way as to maintain our power over women and over the classes below us.* "Competitive masculinity" defines how men must work together.

Competitive masculinity means being productive, materialistic, super-rational, aggressive, power-hungry, authoritarian, unemotional, tough, or, as Third World Gay Liberation and the Gay Liberation Front (both of Chicago) put it: "Male Values are societal values in a male-dominated society; and 'masculinity' tripping comes from the anti-human values of the death culture."[4]

Of course men are not born "masculine." Masculinity is taught, and boys who refuse to learn are deemed not "real men"; they are faggots, queers. Men, like women, are taught to fear and repress our homosexuality. Any man who expresses his gayness is subject to external sanctions. Gary Alinder writes:

I was gay long before I admitted my homosexuality to myself, long before I ever had sex, long before I knew what sex was. When I was ten I played paper dolls with the girls and dug it; when I had to, I played baseball with the guys and didn't dig it. When I was thirteen a gang of four or five guys tormented me—all through junior high school. They called me a cocksucker. I didn't know what it meant, but I knew it was the worst thing a guy could call another guy. They called me *Mrs. Alinder* . . . . I went to a small liberal arts college . . . . Even the . . . fraternity [with the lowest social standing] didn't want me . . . . My gay self was showing through and my gay self was me. And every response I got from the world told me my gay self was despicable . . . . I had friends, other guys at the bottom. I was afraid to be seen on campus with them. I thought I would slip even lower. We were all gay, but that could never be talked about, never be acted out. We were the outcasts, but we were not together.[5]

* In this subsection "we," "us," and "our" refer to men.

Gary's "gay self" is his gentle, non-competitive self. It is this self, this beautiful human being in each man, that heterosexism suppresses. The degree to which a man is "unmasculine," is unaggressive, nurturing, and emotional, is the degree to which he is considered gay by mainstream society. Heterosexism, then, enforces masculinity by calling any man who is not fully "masculine" gay and punishing him for his gentleness.

The man need not be a practicing homosexual. Heterosexism is a double-edged blade. It creates homophobia (fear of homosexuality), and thus succeeds in forcing most men to repress and deny their natural sexual attraction to other men. Imbued with homophobia, each man identifies himself as heterosexual. Society then tells these heterosexual men that they will be called "gay" as an insult unless they also give up the emotional, nonaggressive part of their personalities. Also, a homosexual man may sometimes give up his gentle, nurturing self in response to the pressures of heterosexism, in order not to appear gay, even if he is unwilling or unable to deny his sexuality.

Heterosexism pushes all men to exploit women by forcing men to seek sexual relationships with women which do not deviate too far from the dominant/submissive role patterns and to learn the set of behaviors necessary for dominating—that is, "masculinity." A man who is not "masculine" is not prepared to seek power and dominate. In particular he is not inclined to seek a woman to dominate and control through a sexual relationship. Men punish men for not participating in this system by treating them like women ("Mrs. Alinder"). This indoctrination carried to the extreme is rape. One novel describes a gang rape of a woman in which one man failed to be potent. The other men then pulled his pants down and took turns raping him. Since he had failed to prove himself masculine, he was treated as a woman—and raped. (Notice that "potency" equals "power.")

As part of homophobia and masculinity, heterosexism promotes violence. Next to having sex with women, being violent is the surest way for a man to respond to an "attack" on his sexuality and to prove that he is not gay. Violence, disguised as power, aggression or competition is an extension of masculinity. It proves he is a "real man": "Stand up and fight like a man."

In 1975, the Argentinian government decided to persecute gays on a systematic basis. The following rationale was quoted from the Ministry of Social Welfare's journal:

> As children they [gay men] played with dolls. As they grew up, violent sports horrified them. As was to be expected, with the passage of time and the custom of listening to foreign mulattos on the radio, they became conscientious objectors.[6]

According to Western society, gay men are pacifists—not real men at all—and vice versa. In *Men's Lives*, a documentary film, a high school boy mentions that the other boys think he must be gay, since he is a dancer. Asked why, he says dancers are "free and loose," are not "big like football players," and "you're not trying to kill anybody."[7] If a man is accused of being gay, he must fight to prove he is not; if a man is not a fighter he may be accused of being gay.

In addition to violence, men are taught at very deep levels that we can never be safe with other men. Although men, unlike women, do learn to put ourselves first and to make commitments to men, these commitments are primarily for business and power. Men are conditioned not to have loving relationships with other men. One man wrote after coming out:

> At first I was relieved—they [gay men] were just men—like other men. Then I started to panic. My God! They really were like other men—competitors, rivals, not to be trusted. We could go to bed together—sex between men worked fine—but how [could] we love each other. . .?[8]

Heterosexism prevents men from being lovers in much more than just the sexual sense. It trains us to believe that safe, caring, supportive relationships between men are impossible, and to act in accordance with this belief. The fear of sexuality (and even sensuality) between them keeps most men from challenging this training and stepping through it to connect with other men in real ways.

Submission/dominance and sex roles

We have examined how heterosexism shapes and defines women's and men's lives and how gayness is used as a weapon to make men conform to the male sex role. We began this analysis of heterosexism by showing how it often destroys women's friendships. We have shown that it operates to keep women from making commitments to women and to enable men to govern women's lives. It does so by insisting on clearly defined sex roles.

Sex roles are essential to this society because they are the roles of submission and dominance. This society is fundamentally based on submission and dominance: on bosses dominating workers, on parents and schools dominating young people, on the United States dominating "underdeveloped" countries. Patterns of domination and submission are also intrinsic to the sex-violence of mainstream culture and the relationship of industrialized peoples to the environment ("man conquers nature").

Sex roles are among the first roles of submission and dominance we learn as we are growing up. Though this is beginning to change, it is still true that, by the end of first grade at the latest, most girls have learned to be passive and little boys to be aggressive—the behavior they see modeled in the nuclear family, television, books, movies, and school. Sex roles are also the forms of submission/dominance most entrenched and difficult to attack because they are mixed with love and defined as normal and essential to a happy, stable family life. Men and women conform to sex roles because they are desperate for love and believe that adhering to the established role expectation is the surest way to find a mate. Yet sex roles are clearly the reasons that love takes such unhealthy forms in this society.

Sex roles are so institutionalized that "normal" heterosexual relationships are so unequal, so exploitative, so possessive, so non-communicative, so manipulative, so competitive, so non-respectful, so tied up in power struggle...that a ridiculously unloving standard of love is accepted.[9]

We have seen that men are trained to be competitive and tough and to give orders. Women's sex role is also ingrained: to serve men—to care for them emotionally, sexually and physically; and to seek men to depend on for physical safety, financial security, mechanical skills, and abstract thinking. A woman who does not conform to this role—who develops her physical strength, pursues a career, learns how to repair her car, and/or exercises her intellectual ability beyond the standard currently considered respectable is often called a dyke. (A strong, independent woman and a gentle, nurturing man are both "queer.") Since patriarchy equates discarding the feminine sex role with lesbianism, most women feel a persuasive pressure to be traditionally feminine.

The label of gayness is used as a weapon against "unfeminine" women collectively as well as individually. Many feminists and women's groups fear being attacked as lesbians if they are too militant; that is, if they radically challenge women's sex role. In the late '60s and early '70s many women's groups devoted substantial energy to convincing society that they were not gay. (The lavender herring had replaced the red herring!) Fear of being labeled homosexual has been a successful method of keeping women from demanding all of their rights.

Furthermore, sex roles cannot exist without the repression of homosexuality. Only when humanity is split into two camps, female and male, and love within each of these is prohibited can the emotional integrity of human beings be broken in two and women and men forced to limit and warp themselves to fit their respective pieces. Gay people, gay relationships and gay liberation, threatening the ingrained dominance/submission roles, are profoundly subversive in the present society.

If women and men were freely loving whomever we chose, society could not have two separate castes to which to assign opposite roles. For a woman to have a primary relationship with a woman contradicts her training to serve men, while a man in a primary relationship with a man has no use for training which teaches him to think for women and to look only to women for emotional support. Sex roles are impossible in a society that does not determine relationships on the basis of gender.

However, because today's society assumes heterosexuality and most gays have only the heterosexual relationship as a model, some of us have adopted "role playing," mimicking the female and male roles in relationships. But gays are not very successful in mirroring these patterns. Even when we mirror patterns of heterosexual behavior, we do not become acceptable to heterosexist society. After all, a gay couple, in which one partner acts the female role and the other the male role, is still a partnership of two women or two men and, as such, violates the edict that men must be dominant and women submissive.

You can't do more than pretend to be a man if you are gay. To be a real success you have to do your share in the fucking of women. . . . Of course we can pretend to be like the straight world. We can divide ourselves into imitation men who do the fucking and imitation women who get fucked over, and play all the games straight men play with their women. . . . (But) to the straight world and ultimately to themselves gay men aren't "real men" (i.e., masculine). I used to be afraid of this concept but now I know it's our only hope for survivial, as "real men" drive themselves to extinction.[10]

We are told that sex roles exist to enable women and men to live together harmoniously and to love each other. But actually, sex roles force men and women to participate in the power relationships of patriarchy; that is, they reinforce the control and exploitation of women by men. Heterosexism punishes disobedience to these roles, thus ensuring that most women and men adopt the behavior sexism has set for us and that men exercise power over women.

The connection of heterosexism with other systems of oppression

In this section we will show that heterosexism is interwoven with many other oppressive "isms" in our society, and that each reinforces the others.

Women serving men while men control the world is the central theme of *patriarchy*. Patriarchy must and does repress lesbianism. Patriarchy works with heterosexism to provide each man with an individual woman to service him: keep his house, listen to his problems, boost his ego, satisfy him sexually, and raise "his" children. In addition, the dependence on men *and* the fear of lesbianism generated by heterosexism function to keep women from coming together to throw off oppression.

Ti-Grace Atkinson writes:

Lesbianism for feminism is not just "another" issue or "another" example of human oppression. Nor is lesbianism about autonomy. Lesbianism is pretty clearly about "association"—not aloneness. . . . It is the association by choice of individual members of any oppressed group, the massing of power, which is essential to resistance.[11]

Lesbianism means more than women loving and supporting each other; it means women living, working, thinking, and acting together, independently of men. Such women are no longer servants of men and are therefore in a position of strength from which to develop the analysis, vision, and strategy necessary to attack patriarchy.

It is precisely this very real and substantial threat to patriarchy, women coming together as women and breaking the old ties to men, which enforced heterosexuality seeks to prevent. In fact, we can see that heterosexism is, as the word indicates, a particular and very important form of *sexism*, because its primary function is to ensure that men wield power over women.

We have seen that men are prevented from loving each other, are taught to seek power and to dominate, and are forced to be "masculine." It should be evident that this is crucial to patriarchy; for patriarchy is the perpetuation and expression of "masculinity" in all societal structures and values, and the systematic domination and control of women by men: economically, socially, sexually, spiritually, emotionally, physically, politically. The institution of heterosexuality socializes all men to participate in and uphold patriarchy.

"Masculine" values, especially domination and power, help maintain *imperialist* attitudes. It is no coincidence that we speak of "the rape of the Third World" when the ultimate form of enforced heterosexuality is rape. The United States possesses and uses the Third World in much the same way that men are taught to possess and use women. In fact, the attitude that women must learn sex from men is analogous to the attitude that the Third World must learn freedom and progress from the United States: both are imperialistic. In both instances men claim to bring a great gift (sex, freedom) which will enrich the receiver (women, the Third World) and instead perpetrate violence on the receiver for men's own benefit (sexual satisfaction, economic gain).

Imperialism cannot exist without violence. Violence, as we have seen, is promoted as the second best way, after sex with women, to prove that one is a "man." Politicians claim that the United States must not be weak or timid (i.e., gay); it must defend its manhood, prove its strength and virility. As a picket sign read (after the May 12, 1975 Mayaguez incident in which the United States, with no real effort at negotiation, bombed Cambodia following the seizure of an American ship): "Our nation is safe; Ford has his seamen back." (Henry Kissinger felt compelled to deny publicly that the United States was out to "prove our manhood.") Or, as political scientist Richard Barnet wrote:

> The man who is ready to recommend using violence against foreigners, even where he is overruled, does not damage his reputation for prudence, soundness or imagination, but the man who recommends putting an issue to the U.N., seeking negotiations, or —horror of horrors—"doing nothing" quickly becomes known as "soft." To be soft—that is, unbelligerent, compassionate, willing to settle for less—or simply to be repelled by homicide, is to be "irresponsible."[12]

Although we cannot prove that one depends on the other, clearly militarism and heterosexism strengthen each other by reinforcing similar attitudes. In addition, the gentle, nurturing aspects of men ridiculed by heterosexism are precisely those qualities which, when allowed to develop, lead men to oppose violence.[13]

It may be that one function of *racism* is to channel men's violence. Racism channels white men's violence against Black men, thereby preserving the appearance of law and order in white communities. Black violence is usually confined to Black communities, where it is ignored by white society. Racism, then, helps white society hide the contradiction between "violence is manly" and "a good society is a peaceful society."

Furthermore, as oppressed minorities (in the United States), people of color are treated much the same as gays: their existence is denied, their history and herstory are ignored, their experience and needs go unrecognized, and their identity is the subject of prejudiced jokes and statements. Both minorities are targets of sexual myths; hence we have the exaggerated virility of the Black male, the endless orgies of the child-snatching gay. Both groups are considered less than human, are hired last and fired first, and become a "safe" target for violence. Racism and heterosexism reinforce each other because their methods are similar.

"Masculine values"—competition, materialism, productivity, domination, and power—are also "*capitalist* values." In fact, heterosexism, by repressing the gentle nurturing aspect of men and promoting the opposite, teaches us that capitalism is natural and that socialism, which values equality, cooperation, and selflessness, is against human nature.

The capitalist economy benefits from sexism and heterosexism. Women's role as supporters of men provides for maximum economic exploitation of both sexes. The woman at home maintains the man: she keeps the household and family functioning by acting as a chauffeur, a cook, a maid—and, importantly, acts as a safety valve by listening to his problems and boosting his ego, so that he can work hard and long and accept the boss's authority without rebelling. Of course, the woman is not paid for this work—the capitalist gets the woman's labor as a "free bonus" by hiring her husband. Also, the man, because he has power over some women, within and outside the family, is less resistant to the capitalist's power over him.

In addition, capitalism as a system creates alienation in work, education, and community—especially for women, whose bodies are exploited as sex objects in advertising. Historian Rosemary Radford Ruether emphasizes the way in which the sexist role division establishes a "private sphere"— the home—and a "public sphere"—the world of commerce—and legitimizes two kinds of morality so that the ethics of compassion become privatized and restricted.[14]

Capitalism requires a portion of the labor force that can be hired and fired at will. When the economy is flourishing and the demand for products and services is high (that is, when the people and/or the government are spending money), industry must be able to hire additional workers cheaply. It must also be able to lay off these new workers during a recession without greatly reducing the population's buying power or causing the unemployment figures to skyrocket, and without creating economic unrest. In order to function smoothly, capitalism needs a readily available source of workers who are willing to work for low wages and to accept prolonged unemployment.

Women are ideal for filling this economic niche. Since a woman's work in the home is unpaid and she is supposedly attached to and supported by a man, she can be hired cheaply and laid off easily. Her husband (or, failing that, welfare) will usually support her when she is not "working." (Lesbians and single women violate this pattern.) Thus the traditionally sanctioned institution of marriage helps to establish women as "the reserve army of the unemployed." Capitalism also enforces heterosexuality by making it economically difficult for women to survive alone.

All this strengthens the *nuclear family*. Because of the strictly defined roles to which mother, father, and children must conform within it, and because of its demand that one or two people meet all of one's intellectual, spiritual, emotional, social, sexual, and material needs, the nuclear family can be stifling to many people. Within it, children are taught to respect authority, follow rules and imitate sex roles so that they'll become just the sort of "good workers" capitalism needs. In addition, because it is a small, supposedly self-sufficient unit, the nuclear family encourages high domestic consumption: each family "must" have its own refrigerator, washing machine, television, car, children's playthings, and so on. The nuclear family is vital to capitalism and patriarchy because it produces "good" workers and high consumption and helps men to control and exploit women.

Ageism, in which the nuclear family is a major force, gives substantial aid to heterosexism. (Ageism is not just an attitude: it's the laws and institutions, too, under which young and old people are devalued, cast in limiting roles and discriminated against.) Ageism denies young people self-respect and the ability to make decisions about their own lives. Anti-gay attitudes and behaviors are taught to young people in schools and families where they are not allowed to protest them. Parents of young gays often want to "cure" them and force them to receive psychiatric "help"; they also often forcibly separate their child from her/his gay lover(s) and friends. Gay people below the legal age and/or living at home have great difficulty in resisting such attacks.

There is no honor in the present society for women as they grow older: their experience is not respected, their wisdom is not sought. A heterosexist society devalues a woman who is without a man, especially a middle-aged woman who is considered to have "lost her looks" and is no longer in the sexual marketplace. Because men die younger than women, many older women are widows and suffer loneliness, but heterosexism tells them they cannot be intimate with other women of their age.

Thus we see how the oppression of gays relates to oppression of women, of Third World peoples and countries, of workers and of old and young people. Our society is a web of oppressive systems. Heterosexism, as part of this web, supports and is supported by all the rest.

Class and classism

The class system which has arisen under capitalism is an important part of this oppressive web. Because we think it has special significance, we want to discuss it in greater detail here and clarify how gays and lesbians fit into it.

A class society is one in which people are categorized by where they fit into economic production. The two most basic classes are owners of productive facilities and money (like factory owners and bankers) and non-owners (those who work in places or with tools owned by others). We call that way of looking at classes the most basic because of the importance of power; the owners have a lot of power in deciding the way society goes in a day-to-day way, and the workers have the potential power (through withholding their labor) to stop the economy.[15]

We often don't see this basic class distinction as we live our lives, because the broad group of non-owners is subdivided into smaller groups: "blue-collar," "white-collar clerical," "professional," "housewife," and so on. Over 90 percent of the U.S. labor force makes its living from facilities and tools that others own, but most of us don't think of ourselves as part of the 90 percent. We identify ourselves as truck drivers, schoolteachers, secretaries, janitors, nurses, mineworkers, supervisors, factory workers, artists, and so on, and lump these occupations together with labels like "working class" or "middle class."

These sub-groups that provide our basic economic identity are themselves arranged on a ladder of prestige, so that we look down on or look up to each other according to our occupations and the money and style of living that go with them. That is "classism": valuing and treating people differently according to the class of which they are a part. Like racism or sexism, a classist attitude causes us to overlook the unique human qualities of a person and stereotype her or him according to one feature, in this case the way s/he acquires money and the educational level and lifestyle it can buy.

One of the ways the owning class influences the economy in order to get a larger financial return is by maintaining the surplus labor pool already mentioned. Outright discrimination in education, hiring and promotion, certain laws, and internalized oppression exclude many people from stable employment. Thus, large numbers of Blacks and other racial minorities, "illegal aliens," women, youths, older people and those who are physically different (disabled) become members of the surplus labor pool. In 1981, 44.9% of Black youths aged 16 and 17, and 15.5% of all Blacks over the age of 16 were unemployed.[16] Housewives are kept out of the labor market, except when they are needed, because they are led to believe that their "real place" is in the home. In 1981, 1,237,000 women stated that they wanted jobs but were not looking for work because of "home" responsibilities.[17]

People who are excluded from the primary labor force must, of necessity, take whatever jobs are made available to them—generally high turnover positions that pay below the going wage and require little training. The threat that these people might be allowed into the main body of the labor force makes those on the bottom rungs of the economic ladder (in this country, non-unionized wage workers, often in the service industries) afraid to demand "too much" in terms of salary or job benefits, because they know that they can easily be replaced by the presently unemployed "surplus labor force." Warned that others are after their jobs, workers are set against each other; for example, white workers are pitted against workers of color, Gentiles against Jews, men against women, heterosexuals against gays, and so on.

The reality is, of course, that there is far more than enough work—human, humane, life-affirming work—that could be done, but which doesn't bring enough of a profit to the owning classes to make such work worthwhile to them. Providing adequate child care and health care, building parks and playgrounds, organizing art projects for neighborhoods, and cleaning up lakes and streams is work that would enable all of us to live comfortably and in harmony with the environment. All of these could happen were it not that the economy is oriented toward providing the wealthy with as much financial return as possible.

In addition to restricting *who* works and how much they earn, the ruling class also has much to say about where our money goes. After we have bought and paid for the necessities of life—food, clothing, shelter, transportation, medical care—the money that is left is known as "disposable" income. Of course, there is much leeway in how much of our income goes to the necessities of life—what kinds of food we choose to eat, whether we live alone or with others, what kind of clothes we wear, whether we own a car or not. At the same time, there is advertising, a huge propaganda campaign always underway to help us determine where to spend our "disposable" income. We are urged to spend our money on such things as "better" cars, stereos, vacations, houses, designer-brand clothes, and so on. All of us are encouraged to believe the myth that, if we work long enough and hard enough, and have faith, we too can achieve the American Dream: we can pull ourselves up by our bootstraps and become a part of the owning class, one of the "pillars of society."

How do lesbians and gays fit into this structure? We often accept the trappings of materialism in an effort to be accepted, and we are often shunted into certain kinds of jobs and into high-rent ghettos.

The trap of seeking to increase our status through the purchase of things is a particularly easy one for gay men and lesbians to fall into, as we want so much to be accepted into this society. Many of us believe that if we act "normal" enough we will be able to escape the oppression. In addition, many advertisers now view the gay community, especially the gay men's community, as a desperately needed new market, so the pressure to consume is on. *Business Week* reports that gays control 19 percent of the nation's disposable income.[18]

Particularly in the gay men's world, there is a stereotypical, consumer-oriented "gay lifestyle" where two men live together either in their chrome-and-leather-furnished new condominium, or in their older house with stained glass, natural woodwork and antiques. (This is possible because men are paid more than women: two single men might easily have a combined income of $30,000, whereas the combined income of two women is likely to be substantially less, particularly if there are children to care for.) Surrounding ourselves with these things does little beyond give us a false sense of belonging and economic security, and leaves us numb to the working conditions under which our material goods are produced or to what this consumption-oriented life is doing to the environment of our world.

Gay people come from all layers of society, in roughly proportionate numbers. The myth, though, is that gays and lesbians belong primarily to the middle and upper classes. This is partially because of the highly visible consumption already mentioned, as well as the fact that many lesbian and gay spokespersons over the past ten or fifteen years have appeared to be the daughters and sons of the middle or upper class. What is true is that most gay people are working class in background.[19]

The ways in which gays are treated differs depending on what class they're from. For example, there are some ways in which it is easier to be open about one's gayness as a working-class person: there is generally less to lose economically if one is near the bottom. However, there may be a greater risk of losing friends and family. An owning-class person, on the other hand, is not only much more likely to have financial resources upon which to rely but also is more likely to be accepted socially in spite of deviating from the norm, because of having more power in this society.

Once we have made the choice to be open about our gayness and lifestyle, we often end up in certain types of jobs. This is partly because in some jobs there is a certain amount of freedom from sex-role stereotyping (men as hospital workers, childcare workers; women as taxi-drivers or construction workers) and partly because the public expects many people in certain occupations to be gay (waiters, actors, hairdressers, dancers, etc.).

Jobs that are available to lesbians and gays are primarily blue collar or service-oriented. Middle- and upper-class jobs are not easily available to openly gay people. There are some jobs which it is difficult or illegal for gay people to obtain: school teacher, clergy-person, doctor or nurse, elected official. We are kept out of these jobs usually from fear that hiring someone openly gay would drive away business, or that we will corrupt non-gay people to our way of thinking or our way of life, or that we will physically molest people left to our attention—children or patients. (The myth of gay molesters persists despite several studies which show that the overwhelming percentage of molestation is of girls by heterosexual men.) Most lesbians and gays are subject to harassment at work if they come out there, and that fear influences our ability to get better paying jobs.

. . . and what that does to you is at all times you feel that the world is moving for heterosexual people—that even in the schools everything is towards the family, towards raising children, towards things that are considered normal. This made you feel that you weren't normal, that you were outside society and couldn't be a contributing member, that you couldn't reveal your innermost things, that even on the job. . . . For example, if you had been in a bank as a teller, you felt, "I really cannot advance because if I advance they may find out more about my life, and it will reveal that I am a homosexual!" So on jobs people actually accepted lesser work where they would not be exposed. And in personal life with other people—families, landlords and straight people—they felt they had to play the constant game of not being themselves. We always had to remember that one closet door was there, and it was closed and couldn't be opened . . .[20]

Because gayness cuts across all the class lines in this culture, gays have the potential for building allies across those lines. As we each begin to get clearer about our class background (what our parents did for money, with what privileges, resources, or limitations we grew up—giving us a basic set of attitudes and behaviors that we carry with us throughout our lives) and to take pride in what is good in that background, we can reach out to others both similar and different, from a position of confidence and power. We realize the natural alliances that exist between lesbian and gay movements and the working class, people of color, elders, young people, and others, because lesbians and gays are a *part* of every group and because as a group we share many experiences in society with other oppressed groups.

Chapter III

Breaking Free:

A Vision of Sexual Liberation

"If you don't know where you're going, any road will get you there." It is important for us to describe at least in broad outline the kind of society we think will liberate gayness. Creating a vision will test our assumptions, force us to be honest about our dreams and hopes, and give us courage. Nearly everyone who struggles for change does have an idea, however hazy and implicit, of the kind of society s/he would like to live in. By making our vision explicit, we put it in the public arena where it can be challenged, changed and developed. We expect it to change, because we ourselves are changing. But we are proud of the thinking which has brought us to this point right now.

What is sex for?

In the new society we envision, sexuality will be independent of the biological function of reproduction. Children will be born because they are wanted rather than because they are by-products of a sexual drive.

There is a lot of confusion on this question. Some thinkers, both religious and non-religious, maintain that sex is for reproduction and nothing else. It is as if someone noticed that hearing is essential for the survival of humanity (it alerts us to danger and enables us to communicate quickly to get out of trouble), and then concluded that hearing is justified *only* for material survival; no music or conversation allowed!

Human beings are in fact cultural creatures who take what we are given biologically and create fantastic structures of meaning for our souls: plays, operas, symphonies, poetry, films, sculpture. Those who would like us to reduce our sexuality to reproduction of the species are limiting our potential as human beings.

Even biology does not support the minimalist definition of sexuality; the existence of erogenous areas of the body some distance from the genitals contradicts the supposed focus of reproduction. With women it is especially clear that sexual pleasure is distinct from reproduction. The act of intercourse is important for conception but not for female orgasm. In fact, nerve endings are situated so that most women do not achieve orgasm through intercourse but through stimulation, direct or indirect, of the clitoris. The central place of intercourse in today's heterosexual lovemaking is a result of patriarchal conditioning.

At present sex is often linked by men with domination and violence against women (and occasionally against men). Pornography and advertising objectify women and use images of us as the passive recipients of sex and/or violence. Rape and the sexual abuse of children are commonplace; the fear of rape is known by almost every woman. In the new society this must change: rape, sexual abuse, sexual harassment, battery, forced sterilization, and forced pregnancy will be eliminated along with other manifestations of the male domination of women.

Currently sex is made to serve as a cover for non-sexual needs. For example, all human beings need physical affection, but in some societies, including the United States, intimate touching for adults is almost taboo except as part of the sex act.[1] As a result, most of us have no doubt used sex to get the cuddling and touching we need. Also, sex is sometimes used to compensate for one's frustration in a job or for disappointments in other areas of life. It can be a distraction, an escape from boredom.

Sexual activity can also be an effort to meet a need that was never met in childhood and thus feels endless, so that no matter how many times the adult seeks satisfaction, the need never feels filled. For example, a girl who failed to get the love and attention she needed from her father may as a woman go from man to man seeking this love. Though no man can take the place of her father and satisfy the unfilled "frozen" need of her childhood, she can become free of the compulsive part of that need by expressing and releasing the hurt feelings that have been stored inside her.

In the new society we envision, people will recognize non-sexual motivations and deal with them appropriately. Sex will be reserved for enriching our lives and for deeply touching the reality of our own and others' humanity, as well as for creating new lives through reproduction. We will understand that sex is a way for all of us, of both sexes, to love, play, and reach outside ourselves.

Furthermore, we envision a society in which each person will grow up knowing, enjoying, and having confidence in her/himself as a sexual being. Young people will not be punished for, or discouraged from, masturbating. For people of all ages, masturbation will be seen as a way of relaxing, playing, healing, nurturing, and loving oneself. Making love to oneself will be understood as different from—but not less than—making love with a partner.

Sensuality and sexuality

In the new society sex will be regarded as clean and wholesome. This is difficult now because of the puritanical conditioning we have received. Part of that conditioning is the gap between sensuality and sexuality.

Babies are usually held and fondled. Indeed, babies not cuddled often become physically and mentally retarded—some even die for no apparent reason. Children are still cuddled as they are growing up, but as they reach puberty the affectionate touching by adults usually decreases or stops completely. The Great Anxiety sets in: when and how will the child act sexually with others? Puberty, a time of rapid body changes, when the young person especially needs reassurance that his or her body is okay, is instead a time when s/he gets messages from adults that it is not.

Some teen-aged young people do fondle and hug each other, but sexist messages interrupt such affection by teaching boys that they should be "on the make" and constantly trying to achieve sexual intercourse. Thus they come to see sensual pleasure as a mere stepping stone to that great trophy of masculinity, penetration. The sex roles that teen-aged people play work against the natural affection and support that they need during such an uncertain time. Homophobia, in themselves and others, often prevents them from getting physical warmth from their friends of the same sex.

The Great Anxiety adds to the pressure. In some circles the pressure is to avoid intercourse as long as possible lest one sin or lose status; in others it is to have intercourse as soon as possible to gain status.

The way sexual expression is distorted by this culture compounds the problem, since the preoccupation is with performance, the genitals, and orgasm. Men especially have used sex as a means of releasing accumulated tension, and they often bypass the sensual experience of sex by driving as quickly as possible to orgasm. This is like the production orientation of capitalism: one must pay no attention to the process or to the nature of the activity but only to the outcome which is to be achieved as efficiently and as frequently as possible. Human beings deserve richer, fuller physical delight: playing and dallying, exploring the sensuality of our whole bodies, laughing and crying and being our whole selves when we love each other.

In our vision, sexuality and sensuality need to merge into a continuum, as affection and touching are recognized as necessary and desirable for human health and sex loses its genital and orgasmic preoccupation. This will change the erotic dimension of everyday life in ways we cannot yet see in a detailed way. We sense that flirting will change or disappear. Flirting is often a game which depends on the "naughtiness" of sex; it is a way of adding excitement to everyday activity by sending signals around the edges of it. It is part of romance, the mystification of sex.

Flirting is frequently also a power game, reflecting sexist origins. Since a woman is not allowed to be direct in asking for a date with a man, she is forced into manipulation to get what she wants. This special, romantic form of manipulation found in relations between the sexes reinforces the domination/submission structure in a subtle but powerful way.

The "hustler" behavior pattern, usually displayed by men but also sometimes by women, reduces the potential richness of human contact to a single dimension. By hustling we mean exaggerated charm and aggressive sexiness, conveyed by body language as well as voice, adopted with the intention of getting sexual favors. Friendships can start with sexual interest, of course, but more often potential friendships are sabotaged by the one-track mind of the hustler.

If flirting and hustling diminish, the erotic dimension of everyday life will not disappear. On the contrary, it will be more strongly and directly expressed. We expect there will be simplicity in encounters; that people will be open with each other about wanting to be lovers and will be able to express that without fear or ridicule or gossip by those around us; that we will be free to sleep with each other without that necessarily implying a desire to be sexual; that we will feel sexual attraction without feeling that we have to act on it; and that we will state easily and directly our needs and desires.

Increased touching and physical affection in everyday life may reduce the felt need for intense sexual contact, reduce the domination/submission games which are played out sexually, and enhance our sense of psychological integration.

Same-sex, opposite-sex

As long as we cannot love people of our own sex, we will be trapped by role-playing already set up by patriarchal culture, and we will continue to cooperate in heterosexist oppression. By gay love we do not necessarily mean genital sex; we mean loving with intelligence and playfulness, with physical caring, with sensual delight and with tenderness and strength. In getting in touch with the abundant love inside ourselves, orgasm is not the issue; caring is what matters. Gayness enhances sexual liberation and helps close the gap between sensuality and sexuality.

Same-sex loving is highly validating of an individual's own sexuality. We can identify with and understand the anatomy of our own gender more fully than that of the opposite sex. This is important because a major obstacle in the way of liberated sexuality is the shame and doubt associated with our own bodies. It is also an important way of contradicting the "halfness" school of thinking: that individuals are so many halves walking around seeking another half to become completed. Of course females and males must connect for reproduction, but that should not be the rationale for a crippling self-image. Even many gays have bought this romantic myth. We are *not* halves; we are whole beings who already have within ourselves the capacity for self-realization. We are also social creatures who must cooperate with others for some kinds of production, consumption, play, culture and sex.

Gay relationships are also important precisely because they are not tied to reproduction and the family. They are not propped up by a societal structure (i.e., marriage) which often keeps people together though they don't love each other. This freedom means that they have to be what they are, to stand by themselves as caring relationships.

In all this we are not implying that heterosexual relationships cannot be valid in the new society or help to create new persons in a cultural as well as a biological sense. Whether a person has genital sex with the same or opposite gender exclusively will be an individual question rather than a matter of societal pressure. We expect that the behavior of most people will be bisexual, not because it *should* be, but simply because, with the removal of the conditioning which polarizes sexual choice, most people will *want* to be sexual with people of both genders. But those relationships will be quite different from the models of dominant/submissive opposite-sex love we now see.

Androgyny

In our new society, the images of "masculine" and "feminine" will disappear. These character ideals are made up of human traits which have been distributed between the two genders. It is as if patriarchy took a list and assigned gentleness, nurturing, and cooperation to women and called that "femininity," and assigned initiative, logical intelligence, and physical strength to men and called that "masculinity." Masculine and feminine thus defined are complementary; together they fit the needs of the human beings who are shoe-horned into these roles.

Some thinkers retain the terms "feminine" and "masculine" but try to make it acceptable for men to have some feminine characteristics and women to have some masculine characteristics. We reject this way of thinking because it uses the framework of the old patriarchal ballgame and simply tries to change the players and some of the rules. We prefer to recognize the feminine/masculine dichotomy for the nonsense it is and to abolish it, putting in its place androgyny, a single character ideal to which all can aspire, whatever our gender.[2]

When people embrace androgyny, we will not act out the sex-role scripts which have been written for us; we will be ourselves. Social expectations that are tied to a person's gender will be dropped. The biological distinctions between women and men will be recognized, but all learned, conditioned distinctions will dissolve. Our anatomy will be one more interesting fact about us, not the basis of personality and social expectations.

The new society will encourage and reward in all people characteristics now artificially divided between feminine or masculine roles, such as:

gentleness

nurturance

cooperativeness

intelligence

initiative

being in touch with all of one's own feelings (though not necessarily acting on them)

a sense of identity rooted in being as well as doing

attraction to persons rather than to physical characteristics (no objectification)

sensuality, with appreciation of the erotic dimension of everyday life.

We think these are the characteristics of a liberated person, female or male. Some of them (such as initiative, intelligence) are now allocated to the masculine role and others (gentleness, nurturing) to the feminine.[3] One quality which is fundamental to our character ideal is not strongly developed in either women or men in our present society. This quality is self-worth based on self-love rather than ownership of things or "possession" of people.

A culture cannot say "yes" without also saying "no." If the new society rewards and encourages the qualities already listed, what characteristics will it discourage and confront?

violence

domination

competition

intellectualizing, needless abstraction

selfishness

jealousy

basing self-worth on ownership (riches).

All these characteristics inhibit the love in ourselves and others. The fact that these undesirable characteristics are part of today's masculine mystique gives particular force to the need to struggle against masculinity as a character ideal.

Institutions supporting androgyny and gay love

Desirable characteristics and relationships do not happen in a vacuum. The writers of this paper probably would not even be thinking these thoughts if we did not have a supportive context (Movement for a New Society) for new behavior and new thinking.

The chance to be the kind of people we want to be depends a great deal on the society we live in. If the social environment holds Black people in contempt, shuffles old people into ghettos out of the way of daily business, and reinforces our low expectations of children, then we are bound to have layers of racism and ageism in our consciousness. The fabric of society can be a resilient floor for our individuality, supporting our upward reach for greater love and understanding, or it can be like a collapsed tent, stifling us.

"Society" is, of course, a broad term which actually includes specific institutions that have their own structures and that reinforce certain aspects of our culture. The capitalist economy, for example, as compensation for alienating and disempowering work conditions, has glorified the femininity/masculinity dichotomy, used women as property and sex objects, and glamorized sexuality. It has oppressed gays and then made additional profits from gay business, which in turn increases gay people's feelings of being victims.

Accordingly, gay liberation must mean fundamental institutional change. There is no personal solution to a social problem as pervasive as this. We need new institutions that will work *for* us, that will free the gayness in every human being and put androgyny within our reach.

Androgyny requires that both men and women change. That may seem like common sense until one realizes that programs for social change have often emphasized opportunity for women while tacitly accepting men as they are. The Marxist theoretical preoccupation, for example, has been with how women can change in the struggle for liberation, not on how men can change by emulating women's strengths. Women, Engels believed, had to be brought into production; it was not that men had to become involved with reproduction. He thought that women's family functions of housework, cooking, etc., needed to be socialized, so that women would be free to go to meetings—not that men's identity should be broadened to include domestic maintenance and the freedom to be nurturing and playful. Marxism shows its patriarchal bias here by stressing the value of the role men have played and by urging women to get into that role as quickly as possible.[4]

Here are some of the institutions that will be allied with our humanity:

The economy will provide meaningful labor for all and will be decentralized, socially owned and democratically controlled, to maximize the chance for everyone to lead a constructive life. The cooperativeness and intelligence in all of us will be encouraged and rewarded. Discrimination on any grounds, including gender and sexual orientation, will be eliminated. There will be no capitalist class to take the profits of our labor, to foster division among us, to keep women in the home as a reserve labor pool, and to push men into meaningless work, however, in order to serve the masculine ideal of self-respect.

Egalitarian political structures will replace today's hierarchies, with power for decision making flowing from the grass roots. For example, neighborhood units could meet and make decisions, sending representatives to meet with other neighborhood representatives for decisions that have broader scope.[5] Masculine behavior in the future will not be rewarded by success in those structures. This will reduce the incentive for individuals to develop and maintain masculine styles. It will affirm the cooperative quality in people and increase our sense of responsibility.

Economic cooperation with the earth will replace today's masculinist effort to dominate nature and force her (note: it is "Mother" Nature) to yield more goodies. Technology and decision making will need to be reshaped to be harmonious with the long-run cooperative relationship of human beings with the earth; nurturing is the androgynous quality which will be valued the most here.

A *multi-cultural, multi-ethnic society* will replace the cultural confusion of today. The society will neither promote a "melting pot" in which proud identity gets washed out in mass consumption, nor promote competition in which cultural groups jockey for position on a status ladder with the WASPs on top. Society will affirm the best qualities in each tradition and ethnic group, while also lifting up the common humanity of us all. As Marge Piercy portrays in her novel *Woman on the Edge of Time*, the affirmation of difference and appreciation of variety provide a liberating ethos both for people of color and for gays.

Nonviolent means of waging conflict will replace today's reliance on violence and manipulation.[6] Nonviolent action is a set of tools which brings conflict to the surface but does not usually endanger human life. It is particularly consistent with a feminist style because it combines treating the opponent humanly and asserting one's own needs and beliefs.[7] It holds out the possibility of cooperation later while taking a firm stand in the present. It makes a distinction between the role the person is playing, which is exploitative, and the person her/himself, a distinction many feminists learned to make in consciousness-raising groups, and which Blacks and their allies made in the Civil Rights struggles under the leadership of Martin Luther King, Jr. Finally, nonviolent action contradicts the John Wayne image through which this culture glues together masculinity and violence, the tough he-man who coolly destroys opponents and dominates women.

Non-elitist, decentralized cultural institutions will replace today's competitive and hierarchical world of the arts. The new emphasis will be not only on how well the artist *does* her/his art, but also on how well s/he shares the skills, and on how supportive the art is to the values of the new society, including androgyny. We are not suggesting that an artist who continues to portray love as a flow only between the opposite sexes will have her/his work suppressed, but simply that it will not be as highly valued as it is today. There will be a corresponding change in the relation between performer and audience—art forms will include more participation, and support for growth and risk-taking will replace the narrowly critical view which keeps performers locked into specialties. The distinction between art and life will also be blurred, with more encouragement for creative and perceptive *doing* by everyone, not just experts.[8]

A loving circle of friends will replace the nuclear family as the basic unit of social life. They already exist in some parts of the lesbian and gay male communities as a stabilizing and supporting network for individuals. The members of these friendship circles may or may not live together. They may or may not include a sexual dimension in their friendship. They may perhaps include monogamous pairs or, at the other extreme, let sexuality be a common bond between them.

Communal child-rearing will replace the nuclear family as the typical unit for socialization of young people. Communes will provide a place of growth for adults as well as children, and this will reduce the rigidities between adults and children. Insofar as children mature by identifying with adults, they will have a range of grown-ups to know in a caring way, rather than just two. Communes will typically include people in gay as well as non-gay relationships, so the children will know from the beginning that gay love is normal and natural. Some nuclear families may still be formed, but even these will usually be in a strong community context.

Universal daycare will be available free of charge, with adults who have been trained in child development. Children will be encouraged to develop solidarity with their age groups and will be listened to when they speak for their own interests. Education will include negotiation and confrontation skills, so children's liberation can become a reality. Daycare need not take place in school-like buildings away from the mainstream of adult life.

A society oriented toward nurturing and growing will not need to segregate adults who work from children who learn, laugh, play and cry. In our vision, *all* will be learning and working, playing and feeling. Adults and children will see each other as authentic resources rather than as alien groups to be manipulated and then escaped from.

Unisex dress will replace today's distinctions based on gender. As long as women and men dress in unmistakably different ways, the cues are there for different expectations about how we should behave. This does not mean everyone will look the same or wear a uniform; on the contrary, people will be freer to express their individuality through dress.

The personal struggle

We do not expect that building the institutions listed here will guarantee a liberated existence for anyone, however s/he presently defines his/her sexuality. What the institutions can do is support our growth and undermine our competitiveness, our role-playing and our idolatries. We believe that along with the growth of cooperation will come a personal awareness that will one day make categories such as "heterosexual" and "homosexual" seem irrelevant. The role of genital sexual expression may itself decline, no longer stimulated by advertising, competition, status needs and "frozen" needs unmet in childhood. Eroticizing our daily existence, gaining the comfort and reassurance of cuddling and affection whenever we need it, may leave us without a sex *drive* at all.

The goal of the struggle for sexual liberation is not to be driven but instead to be relaxed, free to decide for ourselves when and whom to love, supported by institutions which are on the side of our continued growth as loving beings.

Fortunately, we do not need to wait for institutional change in order to further our personal liberation. We can begin making changes in our own lives, reaching out for the support we need while we are doing so. Even though none of us can be completely free in an oppressive society, we can each be freer than we are now; being freer ourselves, we can work more effectively for social change. The risks we take and the joys we experience will provide heartening glimpses of what is to be, as well as exciting moments in the here-and-now.

Chapter IV

Five Stages of Struggle for Gay Liberation

We have seen how lesbians and gay men are oppressed, why we are oppressed, and a glimpse of freedom. Now we come to the most difficult task of all: change. Clearly, in order to achieve liberation for lesbians and gay men (and for all people), we need to tear down the life-denying structures of this society and design new ones which will meet human needs and promote growth, love, and equality. To do this requires more than random individual actions or reactions, and more than isolated "solutions" to specific problems. In order to create a new society we must first create a large, powerful movement for change. And for this we need strategy. Strategy is the planning, coordinating, and ordering of our actions for greatest overall impact. Strategy is the guide by which we can direct our energy toward the goal we want.

To develop our strategy we must study the forces which have been used to create change in the past and assess the strengths and weaknesses of the system and of ourselves in order to understand how to generate the power to create change. Then we must sketch as fully as we can an overview of how we should move to bring about a new society. Our overall strategy for fundamental change will then provide a context and a perspective from which to plan and evaluate our actions.

In Movement for a New Society we have found it helpful to think of struggle for fundamental change as proceeding through five stages:

1. cultural preparation
2. organization building
3. nonviolent direct action
4. mass political and economic noncooperation
5. the transfer of power to new institutions.[1]

This general framework is based on the study of many social movements, their successes and their failures.[2]

As we apply this strategy for change to gay liberation, we are aware that it is not a rigid chronological progression. Though on the whole the earlier stages must precede the later ones, the movement progresses in a cyclical rather than a linear fashion. For example, the creation of Olivia Records (a national women's recording company) could not have happened until cultural change had created a demand for proud lesbian music. Then, as Olivia Records grew, it encouraged more musicians to produce albums and give concerts, with the result that more women have been introduced to this music. Thus, building Olivia Records has accelerated, deepened, and widened cultural change among lesbians.

A look at the five stages will give us insight into what we need to do to strengthen our gay liberation movement.

Cultural preparation

In this first stage, gays change our images of ourselves and of the nature of our oppression. The ways to do this are many: consciousness-raising groups, newspapers and magazines, guerrilla theater, seminars and workshops, films and plays, conversation and peer counseling.

Cultural preparation is essential for any group's liberation, but for gays it may take longer and need to be more profound since, unlike Jews or Blacks, we are reared in families of an alien culture. Since almost none of us have openly gay parents, our role models are heterosexual and the values we absorb when we are tiny are heterosexist. We cannot discover our roots as gay people by investigating our personal ancestry, nor are we usually surrounded by our own (gay) people in childhood.

The visiting policeman at nursery school was attractive and impressive; four-year-old Peter got a crush on him. Peter walked up after the presentation and asked the policeman for a kiss. The officer stiffened, then thrust out his right hand. "Boys don't kiss," he said. "Boys shake hands."

Because gays are brought up with myths and put-downs, a high priority is to change our images of ourselves. Political change cannot be thorough without this. The low self-image which has been internalized to some extent by every gay person undermines and subverts our best efforts. We all know that we have acted most effectively at times when we were most self-confident. Personal growth should therefore be on the agenda of every gay organization, whether it is a national civil rights group or local study group.

To develop gay culture and to support personal growth put people within reach of that authentic joy which is what is implied by the word "gay." As the hurts of the past are left behind, lesbians and gay men can feel safe to give up role-playing and to let our gay sunshine come through all the time. This is not to say that we can be fully free while society is still fettered; we cannot. It *is* to say that gay people deserve and can have the rewards of personal growth while engaged in the social struggle.

In the cultural preparation stage, gays can develop a vision of what a liberated world will look like. A vision helps to inspire us, is a force for unity, and guides strategy. It also reduces the chances of cooptation into the present society—the temptation for gays to settle for toleration and the "take-a-gay-to-lunch" response of heterosexuals or to regard even elementary civil rights and superficial friendliness with gratitude.

A gay coffeehouse in Amsterdam:
"Yes," he said, "we Dutch gays have it really good. There is general tolerance all over, but especially here in Amsterdam."
"And how do you feel, yourself, as a gay man?" I asked.
"Well, I must admit that the Christian view is after all correct: I am a sinner." He looked down at the table. "There's no getting around that."

When gays are clear about a vision of liberation (such as the androgynous society we describe in this book), we will be less willing to settle for acceptance of heterosexual people in a heterosexual world and more willing to believe in ourselves.

Such a vision of a new, freer society guides us in our present behavior; it hints at what a new lifestyle would be like.

Josh, who is eight, recently fell in love with Derek, who is nine. Josh wanted to sleep with Derek, to touch him and to spend a lot of time with him. Derek was frightened. Derek's parents saw what was happening and knew how they would like things to be in a liberated world; they encouraged Derek to share his fears with them and to release his anxiety. He became less afraid and was soon able to respond to Josh. He asked his mother to make a sign in calligraphy to put over his bed that said, "Derek and Josh," and he often sleeps with Josh. Recently he confided to his mother that he had taken a risk and kissed Josh.

Political work is confusing, especially in the United States, with its conglomeration of classes, races, and ethnic groups. Gay people are located in all these groups and in all generations and cannot therefore derive a unity from membership in one group. But we can unite in building the characteristics of our best and most desired selves: nurturance, gentle strength, cooperativeness, sensuality, initiative and awareness of feelings. Every political program and organizational chart should be evaluated in terms of these characteristics: does it accentuate or diminish features of the androgynous character ideal?

Gays also need to change our larger political analysis. Many people see the farmworkers oppressed by agribusiness, women oppressed by inequitable laws, and Blacks oppressed by racism, yet do not see the connections between these. They do not have a big picture which shows the network that includes capitalism, racism, gay oppression, ageism, sexism and militarism. The fact is that the connections are very strong—single-issue organizing around gay rights is not enough to build safety for us. Together these "isms" form a system which can be changed only by a broad and sustained attack. The advantage of such analysis is that it also shows what kind of alliances we should create in the next stage of social change—organization building.

Organization building

Gay liberation is like new wine—to hold it securely, we need new wineskins. Now that we have changed our understandings of ourselves and society, we see clearly the need for organizations to educate heterosexual society and to prepare lesbians and gay men to act in our own interests.

We need organization to hold and carry forth our new images and amplify our new power. Organization brings us together to share skills, to gather resources, to assess what must and can be changed, to plan, and to act. Organization provides continuity so that we can learn from the past and plan our future together.

Our organizations serve and strengthen the lesbian, women's and gay communities. They give us strength to defend ourselves against repression and to move forward.

Old organizational forms will hardly contain the exciting fermentation of the new consciousness—in fact, they may turn our new wine to vinegar! In general these old forms have encouraged role playing ("I'm the leader, you're the follower"). Our new forms of organization should incorporate the visions of the new society, show others what we mean by liberation, and support us to change as persons.[3]

Building such an organization takes time and thought and tender, loving care. But by developing trust, by self-education, by sharing skills, and by rooting our work in small groups, we can create organizations which involve everybody in making decisions and doing the work. Our organizations will be stronger if we set realistic goals for ourselves, balance our personal needs with our political aspirations, establish clear expectations and commitments with each other, celebrate our successes and learn from our difficulties.

Political growth and personal growth are not separable. Like our revolution, our organizations must address our total selves—provide support and challenge in our personal lives as well as carry forward our political aspirations. We all have resources we have not yet tapped. Organizations can be a source of emotional and physical warmth and nurturance in helping us to develop our capabilities to the utmost.

I never thought of myself as a writer. I joined the Gay Theory Work Group that wrote this book because, as one of a handful of gay members of Movement for a New Society, I knew I wanted to develop my own understanding of gay liberation and the organization's. And I wanted to work with other gays. Our work group (affinity group) discussed being gay, what we wanted to say to whom, listed topics, wrote outlines and decided who would write which sections. In addition, we each said how we felt about writing and how the others could help us. Writing was a struggle, but the others encouraged me, assisted me to express myself, praised my thinking, applauded my writing, and helped edit my work. Now here I sit, rewriting paragraphs written by an oft-published author.

Most lesbians and gay men feel a big need for community. We want to talk, work, and relax with those with whom we share common identity, experience, and pride. The bond we have with other lesbians and/or gay men can form the basis for creating an affinity group (small collective of three to twelve people) for support, study or consciousness raising, and political action.

To start an affinity group, a few individuals need only decide to meet together to explore the personal and political significance of their gayness. In a rural county in Vermont, population 60,000, a handful of women started the first visible lesbian organization. To attract members they wrote a letter to their local newspaper announcing the formation of the "sisterhood of 6,000" (the number of lesbians that they estimate live in the county).

One affinity group may grow into a network by splitting in half and taking in new members or by helping other groups start. A gay affinity group can also be formed to participate in another political movement. For example, Dykes Opposed to Nuclear Technology (D.O.N.T.) in New York City provides support for its members, lesbian visibility, and lesbian-feminist analysis in the anti-nuke movement. Gay affinity groups can work together with other oppressed groups in common struggles. In California a gay affinity group working in a predominantly Black anti-police-abuse campaign changed many anti-gay attitudes born of ignorance and began to cultivate the ground for a Black-gay alliance.

The small size and collective structure of the affinity group provides for face-to-face interactions which enable members to learn each other's strengths and weaknesses, to trust each other, and to give and ask for support. Ideally, the affinity group becomes a solid base on which its members can stand when undertaking the often difficult and demanding political activity which brings us closer to lesbian and gay liberation and to a thoroughly feminist revolution. When we face harassment, ostracism, jail, or loss of our jobs or custody of our children, our affinity group can give us strength.

Another organizational form particularly well-suited for gay liberation is the caucus. Lesbians and/or gay men who are employed in the same place, practice the same profession, or participate in the same organization, be it a church or a women's center, need each other. Coming together as a caucus ends our isolation, encourages us to challenge anti-gay statements, to come out and to demand equal rights. Where a rank-and-file group of workers or a radical professional caucus already exists, gays can work openly within it, place gay liberation demands in the context of other progressive stands, and insist that the entire caucus become a force for gay liberation. Furthermore, a caucus within an establishment institution can build revolutionary consciousness by exposing how the institution perpetuates the oppression of lesbians and gay men and all people. In addition, to avoid becoming coopted or enmeshed in mere power games with the established leadership of the workplace or association, the caucus must keep in sight its revolutionary goals when plotting its course of action.

A third organizational form is alternative institutions—new, cooperative ways of meeting people's needs. They can unite us, educate us, model new-society services, and build a revolutionary base outside of existing institutions. An alternative institution strengthens the lesbian and gay male communities and builds for revolution when it:

—provides a service that is lacking in mainstream society or hostile to gays (for example, a newspaper which provides coverage of the gay community and gay liberation)

—educates and radicalizes its constituency (the newspaper analyzes the conditions in the community, critiques gay organizations)

—promotes diversity and unity in the lesbian and/or gay male communities (the gay newspaper reports on lesbian as well as gay male activities, seeks out stories about Third World gays, gays with children, class issues in the gay community)

—supports and empowers its members and its constituency (the staff members decide editorial policy and help each other learn and improve skills, and the paper encourages readers to involve themselves in political activity).

Many movement bookstores, restaurants and print shops are also small businesses where members earn a living while working collectively. Alternative institutions have proved to be an essential part of building lesbian culture.

Cooperative living—in groups from three to thirty—is also an alternative institution. Unlike most nuclear families, cooperatives provide a supportive family environment where we can be openly gay.[4] By living together and exchanging information and encouragement with gays from racial or class backgrounds different from ours, we build unity. We educate ourselves and our children.

As an alternative institution, caucus, or education and action organization grows to involve more than a dozen people, it can use a task-group structure to keep the benefits of the small, supportive, egalitarian group. For example, Sisterspace, the Philadelphia lesbian organization, has task groups for Education, Children and Youth, Communications, Social Events, Third World Lesbians, and Budget. Each task group sends a liaison person to a core group which coordinates activities. The core group is accountable to the entire membership.

Networks made up of individuals or affinity groups also bring together large numbers of activists involved in similar yet separate projects for exchange of ideas and information, and political and personal support.[5]

An example of a network of individuals is the lesbian network in the southeastern U.S. formed in the spring of 1978. It is "an open group of Black and white dykes living in the South, meeting one another, establishing and strengthening connections, and dealing with common concerns, particularly racism."[6] Movement for a New Society provides an example of a network of affinity groups. Its groups have different foci—gay liberation, older women's liberation, stopping nuclear power, and training for social change—but are united by commitments to nonviolent revolution, ending oppression, egalitarian group process and decision-making, and providing aid to member groups in struggle.

Publications, conferences and celebrations can all increase communication and develop unity. For example, Lavender Left, a recently formed national lesbian and gay socialist network, sponsored a Northeast Conference of Multinational Lesbian and Gay Male Feminist Socialists in May of 1980. This Lavender Left conference brought together lesbians and gay men from Baltimore, Philadelphia, New York City, Amherst, Massachusetts, and elsewhere to discuss "Feminist Socialism and the Lesbian/Gay Movement." Non-affiliated lesbians and gay men and those from many different left organizations succeeded in working together to create the conference. Speakers of many viewpoints were listened to with respect and interest. Caucuses, workshops, and a party provided for face-to-face interactions and establishing personal connections. A cultural evening helped to build community. Racism was the major theme throughout the conference, and a caucus of over thirty Blacks, Latinos/Latinas, Asians, and one Native American met frequently during the conference. This Third World caucus held a conference of its own in the fall of 1980.[7]

Newspapers such as *Gay Community News* of Massachusetts keep us informed of activities in other locations across the country. Celebrations such as the yearly Michigan Women's Music Festival, which in 1979 attracted 6,000 lesbians from across the U.S. and abroad, are wonderful occasions for exchanging ideas, developing friendships and broadening contacts, and for renewing the spirit of individuals and community.

The Weekend

It was the best time.
I could have stayed for ever.

It was sensuous and wonderful
  the water
  cooling my body
  flowing through my hair.

Women all over
  their bodies
  sensuous with beauty.

But for no man to touch.

Singing with love for one another.

This is a poem S.C., age 11, wrote in school the day after the 1980 Sisterpace Lesbian weekend. She told her classmates about the weekend and then read this aloud to them during "sharing circle."

Through these varied means of communication, organizers learn of successful activities elsewhere and borrow from them those approaches that they assess to be useful in their own areas. For example, marches demanding an end to violence against women have been organized in London, Berlin, Philadelphia, Minneapolis, New Haven, Boston, San Francisco, Cleveland, and elsewhere. Inspired by the success of previous marches, each city has taken the slogan "Take Back the Night" and developed its own organization, logo, and demands. This is an organic process in which actions develop according to local needs. Hierarchical national organizations in which individuals and local groups have little initiative usually don't produce the same groundswell of activities.

We think it would be a mistake to press too soon for a national coordinating structure for the lesbian and gay liberation movement or for all revolutionary forces. Such a structure should come only when the grassroots level is flourishing, when enough people are psychologically freed from authoritarianism, and when skills of egalitarian decision making are widespread enough that the coordinating structure can be flexible and democratic.

Unity in diversity is essential for strength. Our activities must address the needs of all lesbians and gay men, including all races, ethnic groups, classes, ages, physical abilities, and so on. Because class backgrounds are often hidden or misunderstood, special attention must go to exploring class and to encouraging working-class caucuses in mixed organizations.

Coalitions with non-gays are desirable and needed. Gay liberation requires social revolution, which cannot be undertaken by gays alone. Even the steps along the way to revolution which involve gay civil rights generally require non-gay participation. Therefore, gay activists should enthusiastically participate in coalitions for progressive change, while also developing the vitality of separate gay organizations. Naturally, gays will press for the inclusion of gay issues in the wider platform, and should insist on that as the price of support of the coalition.

Before deciding to join a particular coalition, we should analyze the power dynamics within the coalition and how committed it is to patriarchy. The Democratic Party, for example, is deeply entangled with the status quo. Its leadership and its big money are committed to capitalism, to militarism, to ageism, and to patriarchal styles of leadership. The Democratic Party is particularly adept at absorbing dissenters without giving them significant power; it has done so with labor, ethnic, and racial groups and now is in the process of doing so with some feminist women. The party in this way helps to bring reformers into the mainstream, allowing some mainly cosmetic changes but keeping the American empire stable.

Confrontation

When consciousness has been raised for some gays and we have joined together in organizations, we are ready for stage three. This stage centers on nonviolent confrontations in which the good sense and human needs of gays are contrasted with the rigidities of patriarchy. The first gay pride marches were powerful demonstrations because walking together openly and proudly was a tremendous act of courage, defiance and liberation. But if we repeat marches and picketing year after year, they become so commonplace that their impact is minimal. By using our imaginations to create actions that model in different ways the changes we seek, we will have a greater effect. In Minneapolis, the Truth in Advertising League, an affinity group of anti-sexist men, modified—with spray paint and paint-filled balloons—billboards which displayed women as sexual objects. In Seattle, members of Women Against Violence Against Women and some anti-sexist men took effective action against rape when they visited the home of a known rapist, spoke to his wife and neighbors and leafleted his place of business.

One useful strategy is the "dilemma demonstration."

At a Rutgers University campus, student gays announced that everyone who wore jeans on a certain date would be indicating that he or she was gay. In response, a fraternity hung a gay person in effigy. As a result the university was stirred to a new level of awareness about gay oppression.

The dilemma created in such an action is this: if the institution allows the demonstration to proceed, that is good for gays; but if it strikes out at the demonstrators, the inhumanity of the heterosexist system becomes much clearer to the public. As we can see by this example, coming out of the closet can serve as such a dilemma demonstration, whether done by an individual or a group.

If the conservative force (for example, an employer) accepts the new visibility of gays, an important point has been won. If there are reprisals, new sympathy can be won for the cause of gay liberation. The point is not, of course, to provoke a repressive response, but instead to set up the action in such a way that, whatever happens, the gay cause benefits.

An international humanitarian organization with hundreds of employees and a nine-million-dollar budget was jarred by the simultaneous coming out of sixteen employees via a letter to the organization. The gays urged that the organization examine itself in order to root out homophobia and to open up personnel policies. The gay caucus monitored the process of self-examination, engaging in relentless struggle, until a year later the organization's changes were signified by an official statement of policy by the board of directors in which the contribution of gays was appreciated.

Designing and carrying out demonstrations has become a craft, learned over many years by activists and now being taught to others by means of manuals and training workshops. Gays can take advantage of this growing lore by attending workshops and reading books such as Richard K. Taylor's *Blockade*, which tells in dramatic detail how a major direct action campaign was conducted and which includes a manual on how to organize nonviolent demonstrations.[8]

Today, lesbians and gay men can celebrate one political victory: through our actions we have shown that we are a threat to the current patriarchal organization of society. The right-wing counterattack and repression of lesbians and gay men is an indication that our power has grown. The current wave of right-wing repression is no fun, but it is *not* a sign of defeat. If we realize this and prepare ourselves and our organizations, we will be able to respond to repression with stronger actions, rather than retreating or turning to violence or allowing ourselves to be destroyed. And we can take the important step of building alliances with other targets of right-wing attacks: Third World people, women, Jews.

There is a danger in this wave of right-wing activity. We might let our fear take over and go back into our closets. Fear is a great enemy, and one of the great tools of repression. The security of locked doors and closets is false—it just means we offer less resistance to harassment. During the closeted '50s, up to 500 gays were arrested each month in California.[9] In 1978, on the other hand, gays who came out and spoke up in large and small communities all across that state were instrumental in defeating the Briggs Initiative, which would have required the removal of any school employee who "advocated homosexuality" in or out of school.[10] This initiative was designed to make people so afraid they would lose their jobs that they would never be openly gay, personally or politically. Because of the visible political unity of lesbians, gays, and supporters, the repressive ruling did not succeed.

Revolution will not come without difficult and dangerous struggle. This is why building strong organizations on which we can depend emotionally and politically (stage 2) is so important to nonviolent confrontation (stage 3). To succeed, we need an active, courageous, united lesbian and gay men's community.

Mass noncooperation

The stage of confrontation, when successful, builds the movement from fairly small groups of activists to a large force. By the power of example, it wins over the hesitant and emboldens the timid. The waverers are also mobilized by the inhumanity of repressive actions from the Establishment.[11]

The right-wing backlash which repealed gay rights laws in Dade County, Florida; Wichita, Kansas; St. Paul, Minnesota; and Eugene, Oregon in 1978 has mobilized the gay community and drawn in the support of most left-wing movements. The Briggs Initiative, which would have prohibited employment of openly pro-gay teachers and staff in the California public schools, and which a Field Poll in the summer of 1978 found to be winning by two to one, was defeated in a November election by 58 percent to 42 percent because its repressive impact was powerfully revealed. Similarly, in the same year, the anti-gay Initiative 13 was defeated in Seattle.

A woman speaker from the California Outreach Group was confronted in a public debate by a particularly rabid fundamentalist preacher. He referred to her as a "pervert" who, it followed, could have no understanding of moral values. She, never one to deny being a lesbian, instead asked for his solution to the problem of homosexuality. His own admission of support for the Nazis' genocidal solution allowed her to convince the audience, including much of his shocked congregation, that such ideas were in fact frightening and reactionary.[12]

When they see how vicious heterosexism is, people who have been seeking an individual solution realize that they cannot be safe until all are free. Our own life-affirming demands, activities, and vision, and our adherence to nonviolence, attract the support of women and men made uneasy by the repression and violence we suffer. Violence on our part, on the other hand, inhibits the growth of the mass movement which is essential for winning gay liberation—and liberation for all.

—Violence pushes the middle-of-the-roader toward the reactionary forces.

—Violence is harder to sustain over a period of time, and when it is defeated there may be a loss of morale among the noncooperators.

—Violence is welcomed by the government because it justifies massive repression.

—Violence makes sympathy for the movement from soldiers and police less likely.

—Violence tends to reduce the size of the movement.

—Violence reduces the chances of a split in the opposition.

Mass nonviolent noncooperation can be enormously powerful. The overwhelming, coercive force which nonviolent action can have under certain conditions is illustrated by the nonviolent overthrow of military dictatorships in various countries. In Guatemala in 1944, for example, a nonviolent popular insurrection forced President Jorge Ubico out of office. Ubico had been dictator for many years and had the backing of the U.S. (He favored the huge U.S. corporation United Fruit.) His spy system was elaborate and he refused to allow civic organizations; even charity and cultural associations were suspect. Arrests, torture, and executions were part of his rule. World War II opened some cracks in the status quo, however, and students took the initiative in pushing for major change. Other parts of the population followed, and Ubico responded with repression. This time his violence did not work; the population demonstrated and began a general strike. Ubico mobilized the army but the killings didn't stop the movement; in fact, more people joined and the people remained nonviolent. The country became paralyzed, despite the continued loyalty of the army and the U.S. ambassador. It became clear that Ubico could only kill; he could no longer rule. Jorge Ubico, "the Iron Dictator of the Caribbean," resigned.[13]

The tactics of noncooperation include the boycott, strike, sit-in, civil disobedience of various kinds, tax refusal, and rent refusal. Because of the John Wayne image in this country equating power and violence (all wrapped up in the masculinity package), most people overlook the force of noncooperation. When more research into the history of popular struggle has been done, we will most likely find that noncooperation actually can be more powerful than violence in achieving positive political and economic goals.

Gay noncooperation cannot be truly massive at this time because the previous stages have not advanced far enough; there are still many lesbians and gay men who do not have a feminist consciousness, who do not see the connections between heterosexism and other oppressions, who do not yet have the skills, organizations, and experience of working together for change. Although there have been many creative "zaps" and demonstrations in the past decade, the confrontation stage needs to go broader and deeper in grassroots America before enough people are reached in a challenging way and are ready for united struggle.

Experiments by lesbians and gay men in widespread noncooperation are nevertheless important. Gays have participated in an organized way in supporting various causes and have had our own boycott of Florida orange juice. This was primarily an unorganized response to Anita Bryant, spokesperson for the anti-gay organization "Save Our Children," who made her living advertising Florida citrus products. Boycotts have the advantage that one does not have to be out of the closet to participate. Anita Bryant's job with the Citrus Commission ended, most likely due to the boycott and gay uproar against her. However, most boycotts and mass noncooperation campaigns need to be well organized, publicized, and monitored, and to have clear, winnable goals. For example, had the Briggs Initiative passed in California, teachers signing a statement defending the rights of lesbians and gay men could legally have been fired. An effective protest might have gone as follows:

Activists in one school district could have quietly collected a large number of signatures to such a statement. Then in the middle of the school term they could publicly release the document and challenge the school district to fire them. But the school district would be unlikely to do so, for to fire a large number of teachers and hire replacements for them in the middle of the school year would greatly disrupt the "educational process"—not to mention the bureaucratic process. Furthermore, a large number of firings might outrage parents and other citizens, who might be mobilized to give mass support to the teachers.

Actions of noncooperation must be greatly expanded and escalated before they can become a force powerful enough to bring down governments. The power of mass noncooperation depends mainly on large numbers of participants. Large numbers, in turn, depend on a revolutionary situation developing in this country—that is, one in which social and economic problems grow well beyond the ability of the ruling class to manage them. Most people will then lose faith in the Old Order and be ready for new solutions.[14]

Parallel institutions

In this fifth and last stage, power will shift out of the hands of the upper class that presently dominates society. Mass noncooperation will make it impossible for its members to rule effectively. Parallel institutions will provide the new structures through which society can be reorganized.

Power will initially be transferred to the alternative institutions and radical caucuses, which will grow through stages three and four and unite with affinity groups, coalitions, and parties in the movement for human liberation. Many of the new institutions will therefore be a maturing of those which have already been developing in the course of revolutionary struggle.

How gay the new institutions will be depends on at least two major factors: 1) how much gay pride and determination there has been up to that point in the struggle, and therefore how gay the overall movement for social change is, and 2) how well gays have built alternatives that are workable, which genuinely meet the legitimate needs of people. Gay institutions need to be clear alternatives to the gray cement of heterosexist role-playing and also full of nutrition for a healthy new society.

Our strategy for change involves not only alternative institutions but also full participation in the overall struggle for change, while retaining gay and feminist independence to enable us to fight against vestiges of heterosexism in the movement.

In summary

The reader can see that we link the struggle for gay liberation inextricably to the struggle—by all oppressed groups—for a new society. We do not, however, suggest submergence of our struggle in that wider process, but instead the intentional and vigorous development of a specifically gay consciousness, followed by mobilization of gay activists into organizations which are strong enough to go beyond propaganda of the word to propaganda of the deed ("confrontation"). (Obviously, some of this has already happened in the United States, but it needs to be more fully developed.)

Consciousness plus organization plus dramatic confrontation equals a mass basis for noncooperation which, in concert with the growth of other liberation movements, provides the chance for transfer of power from the old patriarchal institutions to a democratic, free, and feminist society.

Chapter V

Lesbian Culture and Strategy

Though we have gayness in common, lesbians and gay men are of two sexes, the one traditionally "first" in our society, the other clearly "second." Out of this difference two very different cultures have developed. As our experiences have been separate, so there are special ways each group needs to act for its own liberation. Therefore, in this book we separate ourselves into chapters, though we know that in life we must often act in concert against our oppression.

LESBIAN CULTURE

Lesbian relationships

The cornerstone of a lesbian identity for many lesbians is a relationship with a lover. There are many shapes such relationships may take, from lifelong partnerships to lifetimes of one-night stands, but regardless of its variety, the lesbian lifestyle today centers around the people we* share our lives with.

To say this does not deny the significance of the political analysis lesbians have developed, or the political nature of society's reactions to lesbianism, or the validity of women who come to a lesbian identity out of political conscience—but it identifies the foundation of the entire lesbian culture: our right to love.

The majority of lesbians are not consciously political women who analyze social oppression at every turn; the concrete day-to-day confirmation of our identity is in our relationships with our lover(s). For most lesbians, in fact, our lover relationships are the *only* positive reinforcement available for being a lesbian in a world which denies, ignores, or abuses lesbianism. And so we often bring to these relationships a fierce intensity and unbridled delight in each other, born of knowing just how cold the world out there can be.

Because of this, the individuals in a lesbian relationship tend to bring to each other a very large share of our needs for affirmation and identity.

---

*In this section lesbian women, and sometimes all women, are "we."

Sometimes this sits like a burden on the fiber of our love, causing strains and tears that might not be there if more of those needs were being met in the outside world.

Breaking up can be a shattering experience that threatens us to the core. It is no wonder that a common refrain for women after breaking up is, "Am I really a lesbian?" (In other words, "Am I really who I thought I was?")

Although there is all the variety under the sun in lesbians' attitudes about relationships, a few general observations can be made:

In many lesbian communities there has been a positive value placed on settling down with one partner. The ideal is to find your "other half," and the longer your relationship with her lasts, the better. Of course, these values are transplanted from mainstream society. Since women are conditioned to value a stable home life, commitment, and fidelity, these values are exceedingly strong in relationships between women. This is reflected in the lesbian culture.

On the other hand, perhaps as a reaction to the values of mainstream society, some lesbian communities seem to stress the ability to be non-monogamous, to be totally autonomous people able to give and take love without asking for any security. In such communities women who seek stability often feel judged as old-fashioned and emotionally immature. Clearly, the form lesbian relationships take varies greatly: some lesbians seek casual sexual encounters in women's bars, others seek few sexual interactions.

Overall, lesbian culture places less emphasis on sex for its own sake than either society at large or the gay men's culture, which may also be the result of subtracting traditional male values and intensifying female ones. This atmosphere allows the many women who are insecure about sex or who have been hurt by the violence of sex in traditional society an opportunity to heal and find sexual equilibrium.

The joy and affirmation of loving our own kind can be a heady experience at first, whether women break through the social taboos after a long and lonely time in the closet or after an active heterosexual life. Many women who have had painful relationships with men feel that all their relationship problems are now solved, that they were simply loving the wrong half of the race, and that it will be roses from now on. They are disappointed and confused when many of the same problems come up with women, and they realize that our personal behavior patterns still determine how successful our relationships are. Sometimes we idealize women, thinking no woman would ever treat us unfairly or hold power over us. Women who come out in a political environment may feel this especially strongly, and many have learned painfully that a woman who is a lesbian isn't necessarily a feminist.

There certainly are qualitative differences between lesbian relationships and other relationships. But simply loving women is neither a cure-all nor the cause of all pain. It is women acting on natural, real feelings and encountering most of the same struggles, issues, problems, and joys that come of loving any human being.

The lesbian community

Lesbian culture goes beyond individual relationships, however. Since mainstream society provides no context for lesbianism, we have created our own culture, and its birth has spanned many centuries. From Sappho and her colony on the isle of Lesbos in ancient Greece, through the witches in medieval Europe (nine million of these women, many of them healers, were burned alive),[1] to the communal lesbian households of today, we have come together to share support, comfort, delight, despair, rituals, music, and magic.

Lesbians have always been in the forefront of women's culture because our full energy can be devoted to it. It is lesbians who are more likely to be free of the emotional, economic, and cultural ties to patriarchal society—to develop something different. Non-lesbians must wrestle, consciously or not, with the sexism they experience in full force every day, and with the temptation to keep the benefits they receive from being with men. This struggle has its own joys and drawbacks and results in a different perspective on women's culture and a different level of energy for it.

In today's political movement a more radical perspective comes from lesbians than from gay men, because lesbians know they fight for rights as women, too. If gay men are accepted as equals with other men, they will be on top of the patriarchal system. If lesbians fight only to be accepted as equals with women, we will still be at the bottom. This is why much thinking and action on racism, classism, and the links between oppressed groups have been pioneered by lesbians.

Lesbians are everywhere in large numbers. Lesbian culture appears when some of these women come together to shape an environment which feels more right for us than the one we experience in mainstream society. The lesbian population is much larger than the number of women visible in places like bars or bookstores. But the visible culture focuses the energy of those who can participate, and its existence gives options, models, and hope to those in less open situations.

> Imagine my surprise,
> Now that I have found you,
> And I ache all over wanting to know your every dream.
> Imagine my surprise
> To find that I love you
> Feeling warm all over knowing that you've been alive.
>
> —Holly Near[2]

Urban lesbians

Most large cities have lesbian communities. The first lesbian space in a city is usually a bar—often a gay men's bar which tolerates lesbians. Gay bars, in fact, can be found in towns with as small a population as 8,000. If a community grows, the number and diversity of lesbian spaces does too: lesbian (not mixed) bars; women's centers which provide counseling, information, and referral services to lesbians; lesbian divisions of local Gay Services centers; women's studies programs at local colleges; lesbian resource centers with counseling, coming-out support groups, literature, referral and places to meet socially; women's bookstores, lesbian businesses (carpentry, catering, printing); lesbian coffeehouses or restaurants; and last but not least, lesbian political organizing centers that focus either on electoral politics or on a grassroots approach to more radical issues. The most developed communities in large cities may have all of these, with variations. Smaller towns often have one center which serves several functions.

Once the lesbian community gets rolling, it can grow very quickly. Urban centers become a magnet for lesbians from surrounding smaller towns who have never felt part of a community in their lives. Often the women's businesses (other than bars) experiment with alternative work models such as collectives.

Rural lesbians

Lesbians in small towns and relatively isolated areas confront different issues from those faced by city women. Some women, born in the area, have forged their own lifestyles out of rural society. Some have moved into the area because they simply cannot be at peace in the city.

Whether they grow crops, raise animals, or have jobs in small towns, rural lesbians often face the mainstream society alone in coping with country myths and suspicions about single women, since they often have no lesbian community to rely on. The reward comes in knowing their own strength, knowing just who is an ally and who is not, and experiencing the rhythm and beauty of living with the land. Some common problems are loneliness, isolation, fear of discovery, little reinforcement of their lifestyle, and alcohol abuse.

In some places isolated rural lesbians are forming networks, traveling many miles to meet for support, skill-sharing and fun. In Minnesota and Colorado, such networks have been assisted by organizations in Minneapolis and Denver, respectively. More informal networks develop as lesbians within driving distance find out about each other and are naturally drawn together.

Across the country there are women's land trusts, commonly begun by women in the city who want access to the land. In the Wisconsin Wimmin's Land Trust (a well-developed, typical trust), a living collective stays on the farm, and other maintenance collectives function out of Madison and Milwaukee. Women buy memberships in the land and come there to camp, work on the land and buildings, and enjoy the country. Workshops and gatherings of many kinds are held in spring, summer, and fall. Any woman may come to work, play, or heal as she needs. Male children are welcome at certain times.

These land trusts are important places for women to learn skills, feel their strength, and be out-of-doors in relative safety. As less and less land becomes available and the economy crumbles, they may become significant sources of food for our own survival.

Lesbians of color

(This section is written by a white lesbian, for other white people. It is meant to give the barest introduction to the experience of women of color, from one woman's experience of work, talk and struggle.)

Women of color are given a very difficult choice if they think of coming out as lesbians: to be true to their racial identity or to their sexuality. The experience of most Black, Native American, Chicana, and Oriental women is that pressure from their individual cultures to remain in a traditional heterosexual role is enormous. Women who come out publicly must look to the lesbian community for support, for they are frequently excluded from the culture they grew up in. Faced with this choice, many women do not come out, or do not even reach a point emotionally and mentally where it is a consideration. Many lesbians are trapped in marriages or other lifestyles which contradict their personal needs.

There is some tolerance for women quietly deviating from the heterosexual norm—"mama's girls" who live with their parents beyond traditional marriage age, single mothers banding together in housing projects. Lesbian bars are a gathering place for some women who are willing to be that visible. But there is little chance to develop a lesbian culture with any social or political impact on the larger ethnic group. (Of course, women's specific experience of expression or repression of lesbianism is different in each culture and in different parts of the country.)

If a woman makes the difficult choice to live openly as a lesbian, she has, until recently, been forced to rely on a white lesbian community. Though the lesbian political movement has been a strong leader in dealing with racism, the fact is that the most visible lesbian culture today was developed by white women for white women, and the lesbian of color is faced at every turn with ignorance, racism, and her own invisibility.

There is progress: in the largest urban areas there are bars and organizations for women of color; a Third World Lesbian/Gay Conference in Washington, DC, was held in October, 1979; a march on Washington in the same month was led by Third World women; more writings on racism by lesbians of color and by white women are published; constant effort within the lesbian community has produced a much higher consciousness around race, which has also affected the larger women's and the gay men's movements.

Class differences

Feminism is developing the idea of classism in capitalist society beyond the traditional Marxist/Leninist, male-developed view, saying that the *experience* people in different economic classes have in the culture is important. Strategy and action come from the impact of that experience, not just from brain work. Honest feeling and honest thinking are both part of a feminist approach to class. Since our culture puts high value on money, status, competition, and material goods, the experience of a factory worker's family that subsists on $10,000 a year and that of a college

professor's family that gets $20,000 are different. And this is important
to political action and strategy, even though, according to the traditional
Marxist definition, neither belongs to the ruling class.

Class differences manifest themselves within lesbian culture as well. A
typical working-class lesbian "comes up through the bars." She has her
first contact with other lesbians in a bar, which becomes the center of
her social life—from coming out, to finding a lover, to developing circles
of friends.

The atmosphere of women's bars is generally more supportive than that
of men's, and coming out this way can be a good experience—but it can
also be frightening or dangerous, emotionally and physically. And chemical
dependency blights our community partly because of reliance on bars for
social life.

Middle-class women do often come out through bars, but they may also
have options working-class women don't. A women's center which provides
counseling, coming-out groups, study groups, and musical events often feels
more comfortable to middle-class women, and when one is established
(usually *by* middle-class women), they flock to it. Social life in the centers
does not so often revolve around alcohol, and some places actively fight
chemical dependency.

Once a women's center is established, the class divisions in a community
are more obvious. The activities and values there (study groups, career
orientation, counseling) are often middle-class in nature, and many
working-class women who frequent the bars feel put down by women in
the center. The fact is that many women who spend time at the women's
center fall into classist stereotyping and *do* look down on the bars, thus
reinforcing a feeling of "we're not good enough for them" among women
who go to bars.

This division deepens in many communities to the point that these two
sections of the population rarely cross paths, and suspicion and rivalry
develop. The women's center continues to meet the needs of middle-class-
identified women, since participation is so low from anyone else, and bars
continue to be the only option for working-class women and women of
color.

This is an example of how class divisions work in some places. There
are many other ways the divisions show:

   —Middle-class women in small towns may have the financial and
   emotional resources to move to a bigger city with a larger lesbian
   community. Since working-class women tend to marry at an early
   age, they are more often caught in marriages, economically dependent
   on their husbands, with children to consider, while middle-class
   women are more often single and more likely to be able to get jobs.

   —Some middle-class lesbians isolate themselves with professional
   jobs and houses in the suburbs that they own with their lovers, and
   live surrounded by the trappings of middle-class success, but without
   a sense of belonging or community. Alcoholism, not in bars but at

home, is sometimes the price. Women of working-class background who have acquired middle-class jobs and values can fall into the same trap.

—Some lesbian separatists who attempt to live completely without men, often on land in the country, come from backgrounds that give them the money and connections to do it. In some cases they have come down hard on other lesbians who do not become separatists, including working-class lesbians who don't have the option.

—Because working-class lesbians feel they have little wealth or status to lose by coming out publicly, they are often bolder socially and politically. This has meant that a lot of courageous leadership in the lesbian movement has come from working-class women.

—Most middle-class women have been taught to play by the rules and not question authority. These are serious mental blocks to coming out, along with the possibility of losing money or standing in their social circles. The result is that many middle-class women are caught for years in painful denial of their identity.

Lesbian strength

Have we painted a bleak picture? It's true there is another side to the lesbian story: occasional supportive job situations, loving families, understanding former husbands, lesbians of color who succeed in living in both their cultures or in forming an ethnic gay culture—even some sympathetic TV shows. But these are relatively few.

What is more important is the incredible strength we have developed to withstand these daily pressures and threats. That strength, hard-won and well-prized in the emerging lesbian culture, is an inspiration and a delight, and a reason to be confident that we will win the larger liberation struggle.

SEPARATISM AND SOLIDARITY: A LESBIAN FEMINIST PERSPECTIVE

As lesbian-feminists, we are determined to struggle against patriarchy for our liberation, and the liberation of all women, because we are women who love women in terms of time, energy, and commitment as well as sex—in other words, thoroughly woman-identified women. We believe that gay liberation is but a part of a larger feminist revolution which is necessary to free all of humanity. This section will explain why we think that, at this point in the struggle, separatism is the best strategy to bring about our liberation and that of all women.

The mere mention of the word "separatism" often upsets people, especially men. The concept seems threatening, and incompatible with solidarity or people's unity. We do not think this needs to be true: on the contrary, a good degree of separatism is crucial to healthy solidarity.

Much unnecessary pain and confusion result from the fact that different people use the word "separatism" to mean very different things, without defining their terms. To some women, separatism means a state of (almost) total separation from men, socially, sexually, politically, and economically. They see it not only as a means of waging struggle against patriarchy, but also as the goal: the Lesbian Nation, completely separate existences for women and men.

Such total separation is not our goal; nor is it what we mean by separatism. We see, however, a strategic need for oppressed groups to organize separately, and to *be* separate in many instances. A group uses separate space both to gain strength for the struggle and also to develop and celebrate its own culture—the special things that happen when women, gay men, Blacks, or Jews, for example, are in their own groupings. We advocate this kind of separatism for all groups working for their rights, and for women in particular. The ultimate goal of this separation, however, is solidarity: all people living and loving together in mutual respect. We will need all the power we can muster to pull down patriarchy. This will not happen unless all groups are working together: women and men, gay and non-gay, working class and middle class, people of all races and ages. However, we are not yet at that historical point, and, precisely because of oppression, unity cannot be our *means* of struggle—yet. True solidarity will be attainable only if we initially work separately. Every struggling group needs separatism as part of its strategy. Individuals need different degrees of separatism at different times in their lives and at different points in history, but separatism is vital to every oppressed person.

Each group needs separate space and time to identify and analyze the way it has been treated. The individuals need to build their strength and confidence and rid themselves of self-denigrating attitudes and behaviors which can rarely be seen clearly until one has stepped away and taken a hard look at one's oppression from a safe place away from its constant reinforcement.

Separatism is also important in allowing individuals to recognize how they have been hurt without blaming it on each individual member of the oppressor class. Thus it is especially important for women to have separate space from men, since for women the pain of injustice is tied up with individual men we love or have loved deeply. Analyzing together our situation as women helps us to see it as systemic, and not necessarily the fault of individual men.

Each group also needs separate space to develop and rejoice in its own herstory or history, culture, identity, style, and spirituality, all of which have been repressed by the dominant culture. This is why the development of Black, women's, and gay music and poetry is so important. As Rita Mae Brown has said: "Art is the rising star of the revolution (but no substitute for political power)."[3]

Separate space meets our need to have a safe haven in which to relax, a place where we can regain strength and courage to go back out and tackle the world again. Complete safety cannot be obtained completely in the presence of people who have been socialized into dominant roles, even if they do not mean to be oppressive now, and are trying hard not to be. We all need some place where we know we are not going to have to suffer the discrimination and insults that are dumped on us daily in the outside world.

Indeed, many lesbians who do not identify as separatists practice separatism to some degree. We live alone with our lovers or in women's households, we go to lesbian bars or coffeehouses, we socialize with lesbians. If we work a traditional job, we feel the need at the end of the day to get back to a safe space where we can be ourselves.

My lesbian communal house was extremely important to me in providing a safe place where I knew there were not going to be any sexist men around and that no one was going to make a homophobic joke. Having that space to relax in, I was more willing to engage with men at other times and to challenge their sexist behavior with less resentment.[4]

Sometimes, members of oppressed groups do not have the privilege of this separate space or the power to take it. We must more consciously create such space, and work to make it available to others.

Separatism does more than meet needs for consciousness-raising and provide a safe space. It is the means by which each group can build its power and become a strong political force. Eventually such a group can struggle for its rights in solidarity with other groups from a position of equality and strength. Thus, not only do gays and lesbians need their own separate organizations, but there should be Black, working-class, young people's, and older people's caucuses within them. Since almost all of us are both oppressors and oppressed in some way, we need to be careful as we organize (e.g., around gayness) not to perpetuate other kinds of oppression within our own political groups (e.g., white gays condescending towards Black gays). In the Wages for Housework Campaign, for example, the women involved struggle together for their common goal, but Black women and lesbians have separate caucuses to make sure that their particular needs and concerns are met.

Without the strength, self-identification and self-direction that downtrodden groups can gain by being separate, "solidarity" is hollow, phony, and superficial. "Solidarity" without separate organization usually means that the oppressed group is settling for diluted but continuing oppression, perhaps with the most brutal edges removed, but with the power relations basically unaltered. Women who are guilt-tripped by radical men into working for (male-dominated) socialist organizations in the name of "solidarity"—instead of working at least part of the time for their own cause as women—are falling into just this trap; in the name of people's liberation and unity, they settle for a continuation of sexism.

Working with other groups needs to be a free choice and to come from a gut feeling of connectedness with other people's suffering. It should not be a result of feeling guilty because one sees, intellectually, the need for solidarity but in one's heart resents it. The gut sense of unity with other people's needs is rarely possible before one has had the (separate) space to understand and work on one's own needs.

This is not to say that there can be no useful solidarity at this time. On the contrary, some groups who have had sufficient separate space to come to grips with their own reality are now working together well. For example, gays and some unions in San Francisco have formed an alliance to support each other's demands of City Council.

Perhaps the guideline for being in coalitions with members of a dominant group should be to work from a position of strength. In situations where we would have to take a back seat and would be subject to further mistreatment, either by commission or omission, it is better not to attempt unity at this time. One exception might be to form a caucus of our own within an organization that we are committed to changing. In all cases, there is a continuing need for separate organization as well.

In practicing separatism, it is important to realize that oppressors want us to be divided and fighting one another. To counteract this, we can:

—recognize who ultimately will be allies, even if working together now is impossible because of oppression dynamics.

—explore how to struggle with other political groups without selling out our own power. This includes figuring out how to tell when it's constructive to struggle and when it's damaging or just not worth it.

—avoid actions which will undercut the strength, credibility, or unity of other politically organized groups, even if we disagree with them. We can choose either to struggle with them directly or not work with them and concentrate on our own strategy.

—work in the group on taking strength from separation, not supporting each other to feel like hopeless victims in a cruel society.

—look at the situation within our separate groups. Race, class, religious, physical, and ethnic differences need to be acknowledged and respected as we oppose oppression around sex and sexuality.

—recognize that members of an oppressor group are usually oppressed in other ways (men as workers, Blacks, and gays, for instance) by the same system. This will help us see them as human beings today and may eventually be a basis for unity.

Gender oppression is very, very old. Women were dominated by men long before political-economic systems such as feudalism, capitalism, or socialism arose. This does not mean that struggling against patriarchy is more important than struggling against capitalism, or that the two can be separated. It means that patriarchy is a fundamental system of oppression, not simply a manifestation of capitalism.

Separatism by gender is sometimes regarded, by people who consider capitalism to be the basic system of oppression, as a capitalist plot to keep us divided. We think this is inaccurate and misleading. A socialist revolution that is not also a feminist revolution will not end women's oppression.

Separatism must be seen clearly as the first step in combatting the real and devastating ways that different groups in this society are taught to hold each other down, *so that* we can come together in solidarity to pull down our real enemy.

Separatism changes the lives of individuals

Separatism is not only the most effective way for women to come to understand our oppression; it also helps us to break out of our own internalized sexism (that is, to stop believing the denigrating things that are said about women) and to begin refusing to tolerate men's sexist behavior. Once a woman finds her separate space, she starts to get a sense of what it is like to be her own boss instead of playing second fiddle to the man and his greater power. She sees what freedom might be like in ways she could not imagine while she was still relating to men and still unconsciously accepting traditional men's and women's roles. A separatist woman steps out of the oppressive ways the men in her life treat her; and out of the conditioning which has taught her to be supportive of men at her own expense and to assume second place, to *cooperate* in her own oppression.

With no men close to us, we are forced to rely on ourselves and each other. We can no longer rely on men for status, approval, respect, money and practical skills. It is not until we are away from men that we realize in how many subtle ways we're accustomed to leaning on them. We are forced to realize our own capacities.

Being exclusively with women not only helps us break out of traditional ways of relating to men, it also pushes us to get rid of our sexist training in relating to other women. We can stop competing with each other, hating each other, and considering men superior and better company. The depth of this conditioning is hard to understand until it is confronted in full force. Women who make commitments to each other and identify strongly with each other instead of with men, as in separatist living and working collectives, contradict this sexist behavior towards each other and learn instead to love each other and give each other support.

Women also have an urgent need to define our own culture: identity, herstory, politics, and styles of working and relating. Women grow up in male-controlled, heterosexual families and not in our own culture. Reclaiming the values, intuitiveness, healing, nurturing, and competence of women is like an adventure into a country where we were born but were never allowed to live. Powerful things come out of a women's culture.

After a string of hard emotional experiences, Lily had reached a breaking point in her life that left her unable to cope with the world physically, emotionally, mentally, or spiritually. In the mainstream world it would have been called a nervous breakdown—Lily would have been institutionalized and told she was a sick woman. This could have affected her self-image for the rest of her life.

Instead, Lily's lesbian household and community of friends reversed this image of her experience, helping her see she was going through a very deep healing process. They encouraged her to cry and let out all the emotions she had buried, and not to feel guilty for freaking out in a world that is designed to freak women out. They helped her say "no" to her many political, job, and social commitments, and pay attention to her own needs instead.

Lily relaxed and allowed herself to work through the confusion and pain for a period of months, gradually reestablishing her boundaries and behaviors in the rest of the world, and becoming a freer, more centered person than ever.

What has been a life-shattering experience for many women became a rebirth for Lily, through a combination of an empowering analysis of why she was hurting, and the nurturing energy of women coming together to heal each other.

Defining our own culture is much more difficult in the presence of men, who can be expected to be defensive and critical.

Separatism thus has a very important role to play in providing the support and space for women to break out of our inner sexist conditioning—a liberation essential not only to the personal health and fulfillment of individual women but also to the continuing and successful fight against patriarchy.

Separatism is not inspired by purely political motives. A woman's feelings are important in her decisions about separatism. First there is the fulfillment of loving her own kind:

The first few months of my first lesbian relationship provided continual consciousness raising for me about the oppression of women by men. I gradually became aware of all the ways I had been unfree in my previous relationship with a man, which neither of us had ever identified, although we had struggled long and hard with sexism and I was, by heterosexual standards, a very aware, independent, and liberated woman.

The difference between lesbian and heterosex was shattering; and it was not until I was in a gay relationship and making comparisons that I could identify many of the ways in which I had previously been passive, unassertive, and indecisive. There were so many new areas in which I had to learn to take the initiative.

Women know how to nurture and give back energy to each other and how to love, to play, and to make love in ways that men have generally lost touch with because of the effects of patriarchy. Thus, right now, relationships between women are often easier, more fun, and more sustaining than relationships with men. Many women are choosing separatism, at least in personal relationships, for (rightfully) selfish as well as political reasons.

There *is* a danger for women, however, in the fact that lesbian relationships are often so much more fulfilling than heterosexual ones. Sometimes when a lesbian discovers the joy of loving women, she feels that she has arrived, that she has made it, and that this is the individual solution to all her problems. She is tempted to put more and more energy into her personal relationships and lose her militancy as a feminist. Women in this position sometimes just transplant the values of the rest of society, such as forming isolated couple relationships and competing with the Joneses, into their lesbian lifestyles. It is crucial for a feminist who becomes a lesbian to keep her political analysis in mind and not to imagine her oppression as a woman has ended just because she now has a woman lover.

Women's feelings about men also play a part in our becoming separatists. Of course women have negative feelings about men who treat us badly, and it is healthy for women to be in touch with such emotions and to express them.

One woman in my lesbian discussion group defined separatism as "a general disinterest in the continuation of the male species." I laughed uproariously. My immediate reaction was to identify with the speaker. Then suddenly I saw what I was doing. . . . If I let my feelings rule, I can all too easily equate men's learned sexist behavior with men themselves, and wish them off the face of the earth. I realize how easy it is to let my hurt feelings about the sexist ways men have treated me to confuse my political thinking and lead me into actions that go against my own goals of unity of humankind.

What is important is not to be ruled by such emotions. Anger is no substitute for clear strategic thinking. However, there is no reason why a woman should make it a priority to deal with all her feelings about men. Rather, it is quite reasonable to say to a man:

> I have a lot of feelings about you because of your sexist behavior, and right now it is not worth it to me to work through all those feelings so that you and I can maintain a close relationship. I've spent my life so far putting my primary energies into men and now I want them to go to women. It's not that I don't care about you or that I am punishing you for having grown up a man under patriarchy. You are just not a priority for me, and I know you can get support from other men.

Women have to make political choices about where to focus our energies. Moreover, we can often work through our feelings about men a lot faster once we are a little removed from the oppression. Trying to struggle out from the middle of the fog is harder and less effective. For a woman to want to feel clear about men *before* she separates herself from them is like not wanting to eat until her stomach stops hurting, when hunger is what is causing it to hurt.

It is reasonable to want to avoid being subjected to men's oppressive behavior patterns whenever possible, but it is important not to condemn the male human being at the same time. Underneath the learned sexist behavior most men are good, loving people.

If one goal of women's liberation is unity with men as equal human beings, women need to keep in touch with the fact that men can be beautiful too. And we women can try to keep our actions consistent with that goal and not contrary to it.

Separatism helps build the women's movement

We have examined the individual political changes that take place when a woman becomes a separatist, how she breaks out of her own sexism by changing her consciousness and behavior. However, separatism is equally important in building the women's movement. Separatist women are committed to giving their primary energy to women; thus they are able to build power as a movement in a way that would be impossible if each woman were putting her primary energy into a man.

Unfortunately, separatism as it is currently defined and practiced by some lesbians seems to be counterproductive. Separatists who spend time and energy trying to convince non-separatists to join them, or criticizing women who are "cooperating with the enemy" rather than creating power as a movement, are in a very real sense still putting energy into men, and in a non-effective way, since they do not consider the possibility that there might be men who could be functioning as allies.

The question of energy is an important one. Women under patriarchy have retained the ability to support, nurture, and give back energy; most men have not. Therefore, women can get support more easily from other women than from men. To do so leaves us more energy for organizing and political work. Some women receive enough from relationships with some men that they choose to continue them, but the process of struggle itself can absorb a lot of energy that would otherwise be available for other women. Each woman needs to weigh these things as she decides with whom and how to have relationships.

There are several reasons for this imbalance of available nurturing energy. Both sexes are taught that love, nurturance, and support are finite resources, like oil or coal, that must be measured out, and we all have fears that we will not be able to get our "fair share." Many human relationships become power struggles, with each person pushing to be the one with the most power. Men in this society have been able to gather more of the visible trappings of power in the form of money, status, influence, and access to people and jobs, and some men have more internal power, in the form of self-image and confidence. It is the male ability to project the illusion of great power along with the threat of reprisals (disapproval, withdrawal of emotional and economic support, or violence) that puts many women into a state of powerlessness. Until a woman realizes that she is indeed equal in ability and self-worth and always has been, she may spend a great deal of time and energy struggling with feelings of inadequacy. Relationships with other women, while not always free of power struggles, can often give a woman a chance to break through her internalized attitudes about feeling powerless, and help her get in touch with her own strength and abilities.

We don't need to think of energy for other people as a commodity which women produce and should measure out to people as they see fit. Ideally when we are nurturing and being nurtured, more energy is produced in each of us, and our energies fuse with those of our circle of friends or co-workers until it is a common pool we draw on. If this is happening for a woman with some men, there is certainly no reason to reject that energy. At the same time, every woman can recognize the forces in society which influence her to have relationships—usually with men—where she gets back much less than she puts in.

Women who are dependent on men emotionally or financially feel restricted because of the fear of losing so much (at least in the short run) by refusing to tolerate men's sexism. Women who are not economically dependent on men can take advantage of this freedom by challenging men's behavior and by encouraging other women to develop the skills they need to become more independent.

It is clear, therefore, that separatism for women must play a major role in feminist strategy. By this we mean significant but not total separation from men. Total isolation and independence are impossible anyway; even if a group of lesbians builds a completely isolated self-supporting community deep in the country, the money to buy that land must still either be earned or inherited from the system, and the women are still subject to the laws of the state and the nation. Nor would complete separation be a goal even if it were possible; women will destroy patriarchy by confronting it, not by isolating themselves from it. To quote Rita Mae Brown again:

> An island of feminism can't survive in a sea of patriarchy; or, at least, it can't come to political power.[5]

Separatism must be seen as the means and not the end of feminist struggle and adopted only to the degree necessary; it must not become an obsessive search for any kind of "purity."

Bisexual women

It seems important to distinguish between people who are functionally bisexual and those who identify as bisexual. Many gay people, female and male, occasionally desire to have sex with people of the opposite gender.

This makes them functionally bisexual, although their identification remains gay. The same is true of people who may identify as primarily heterosexual but who may have had some same-sex experiences. A truly bisexual person, on the other hand, is strongly attracted to people of both sexes. Many politically aware bisexual people of this type, especially women, have chosen a lesbian or gay label for the time being because it does not seem to be possible to make a strong feminist statement from a bisexual position.

Bisexuality can be seen as a no-win situation in several ways. Mainstream society may insist upon assuming that a bisexual woman is still "basically" heterosexual, the men she relates to may assume she is more committed to them than to other women. Or they may see her as "kinky," relating her bisexuality to her sexual practices only and not to her political beliefs at all. The lesbians she comes in contact with, on the other hand, may respond to her with distrust because she is viewed as lacking commitment to women, and as giving aid and comfort to the enemy. For this reason many lesbian separatists refuse to deal with bisexual women. The whole question of bisexuality brings up hostility, confusion, and conflict. Bisexuality may be seen as either politically incorrect or, at best, as merely a stage in a woman's coming-out process. It is genuinely difficult for those who are bisexually identified to be taken seriously on either side of the struggle. They have in some ways taken on the best and the worst of both worlds.

It is important to be especially supportive of bisexual women who have chosen to call themselves lesbian, for in doing so they have stated very clearly that they place women's concerns first, politically and personally. To be critical of a woman who has publicly accepted and stood by a lesbian label simply because she has privately revealed that she identifies more closely with bisexuality is divisive and damaging to the unity we need if we as women are to be taken seriously. The larger issue is to unify all women, regardless of their sexual preference, to join in the struggle for liberation. Patriarchy will continue to dominate and separate us as long as we see the issue as one of "political correctness." This concept in itself seems to be cut out of a patriarchal mold. It seems negative to pressure people to label themselves according to a pre-set collection of definitions that may have little or nothing to do with their life experiences. Equally damaging is the tendency to place so much emphasis on sexual practice. We have stated repeatedly that being gay involves much more than who one sleeps with. Being gay and feminist, while it does mean supporting our right to be sexual with others of the same gender, also means commitment, struggle, and having a vision of what the world would be like if we were all free to act on our own feelings of love for one another.

The "more lesbian-feminist than thou" trap or the desire to be "politically correct" can often take as much energy from women as does struggling with men. If a woman has committed herself to other women and spends a good deal of time and energy dealing with women's issues and women's culture, she deserves support even if she is continuing to relate to men in some ways. The bisexual woman, in turn, must respect and support the needs of gay women for entirely lesbian space. Since we as lesbians are not involved in relationships with men, it may be easier for us to see the problems in a relationship that a bisexual woman may be having with a man. We have a responsibility to challenge her when it seems to us that a particular relationship is sexist or otherwise oppressive, but we do not have the right to assume that all opposite-sex relationships are dominated by sexism or that all same-sex relationships are free from oppression. Each woman has a right to choose for herself with whom she will associate and where her energies will go.

Don't Shut My Sister Out

Chorus:
Don't shut my sister out, trust her choices,
Her woman's wisdom and her will to grow.
Don't shut my sister out, trust her vision,
Her intuition of her own way to go.

Well a woman's rhythm is an ebb and a flow,
It's a comin' together and a lettin' go.
Like the tides of the moon and the seasons of earth
We sing our cycle of death and rebirth.

Sometimes I find myself takin' a stand—
It's like finding rocks among the shiftin' sand—
And sisters gather round holding hand in hand,
Saying, "This is our story, this is our land."

Sometimes I find I have to walk away—
There are inner voices that I have to obey—
And they lead me lonely, and they lead me cold
And they lead me away from the sisterfold.

One thing I've learned is never to assume
That every woman I meet is gonna sing my tune.
I want respect, I want to give you the same,
This is a struggle for survival, not a party game.

I see pointin' fingers, I hear callin' names,
I see our strength shattered by fear and pain.
Can't you see the writing on the wall?
If we don't join together, well, we're all gonna fall!

You are a special woman, shouldn't have to hide.
I want to know you, grow with you right by my side.
Won't you come as you are, won't you do what you must,
Won't you help build a sisterhood we all can trust?

—Betsy Rose[6]

There are, fortunately, some men who have worked very hard to free themselves of sexist, racist, and classist attitudes. These men are learning how to nurture others and how to be supportive of women without draining them. We must demand that they prove they can be trusted in these areas by demonstrating these qualities in their relationships with one another; however, we must not deny their existence or require women to give up relationships with such men in order to be accepted as our political allies.

Bisexual women are in a potentially powerful position when they are in relationships both with other women and with the kind of anti-sexist men just mentioned. A politically active, aware bisexual woman can serve as a model for one of the roles of the new society we are trying to build. What keeps lesbian separatists from seeing this and offering bisexual women support and appreciation is our own internalized oppression, both as women and as lesbians. This means, as we have said before, that we have heard negative things about ourselves from others for so long that we have to some degree begun to believe them, and that these beliefs are so ingrained that we have trouble recognizing them as a part of the wider oppression we are fighting. When we are comfortable in our own minds about our sexual identity and our political choices, we will cease to view the struggle as a competition in which each side gains or loses points based on how many people are wearing our label. We will be able to state our own needs and visions powerfully and to accept as valid the needs and visions of others.

We have a responsibility to work through our fears about being politically or personally alone. Then we will be able to give up the notion that love and energy are finite resources and that bisexual women will always give more to men. Once we as lesbians have worked through the old feelings of being helpless and powerless victims, we can assist bisexual women, and the anti-sexist men they relate to, to be natural and powerful allies. We will, of course, continue to challenge them from our position as strong women, but without feeling a need to criticize or invalidate the ways they have chosen to lead their lives.

When I was identifying as a bisexual woman, I found myself in a continual struggle not with the men I was associating with but with the lesbians I wanted to be closer to. I found I was using most of my political time arguing over the validity of my relationships with men and defending my right to be who I thought I was. Even though I had a woman lover, the fact that I didn't feel comfortable with a lesbian label seemed more important an issue to my sisters than the fact that the great majority of my time and energy was going to women. I was continually put in the difficult situation of going to my supportive men friends for nurturing and healing because of the almost continual put-downs I was getting from lesbians who claimed to be feminists. Finally I decided to adopt a lesbian label just to see if it would shut people up. It did, and now I seem to have established some credibility with my former critics, despite the fact that I still relate to my male friends.

Lesbian feminists and heterosexual women

It is important that lesbian feminists and heterosexual women recognize our common oppression as women, see ourselves as part of the same struggle, and be able to work together for our common liberation. Of course lesbians need time to be separate to build our strength as a sub-group within the larger oppressed group: women. Thus we will be able to confront heterosexual women who act negatively towards us and will be able to work with them from a position of strength and equality rather than of invisibility or oppression.

Lesbian and non-lesbian women have many more commonalities than differences. It is to the system's advantage to keep women divided and fighting each other; women must constantly guard against this division in order to build strength against patriarchy. Lesbians need to keep in touch with non-lesbian women all the way through the struggle. There is no place for extended separation of lesbians from non-lesbian women in the way that there is of women from men. Rather, the most effective way to counter heterosexism in women is for lesbians to maintain connections with non-gay women and to keep sharing with them, supporting them and emphasizing commonalities. If this does not happen, heterosexual women's fears along with their stereotypes of lesbians will continue and be strengthened rather than broken down. After all, many lesbians were heterosexual once, and non-lesbians usually need information about lesbians, lesbian support, and above all, lesbian friends in order to get in touch with their emotional and physical feelings for other women.

If we are serious about separatism as an important part of the strategy for feminist revolution, we need to support non-lesbian women in their struggle to become separatists themselves. We must not withdraw into the comfortable company of other lesbians, demanding that non-lesbian women become separatists without helping them to do so. Certainly heterosexual women oppress lesbians sometimes. Lesbians do not need to tolerate this behavior; we do, however, need to take the risk that this behavior will occur and that we will have to challenge it, and not fearfully refuse to expose ourselves to that possibility.

It is also important for lesbian feminists to remember that non-lesbian women are rigidly heterosexual only because of heterosexist training, and to find ways of showing them that this is the case. These ways must be illuminating and empowering rather than aggressive or threatening. If loving women really is natural and joyful, as we believe, then all women will want to love other women, whether or not they become sexually involved. Lesbians oughtn't to try to force other women into it; just keep pointing out the blocks which keep them from realizing it.

Lesbians should think about the support that we give to non-lesbian women and avoid being pressured into doing things which do not make sense to us. For example, lesbian feminists will not want to give to non-lesbian women the support to stay in oppressive heterosexual relationships, but we do want to support them as women, in ways that strengthen and empower them. One way to do this is for lesbians to challenge women who are in obviously oppressive relationships with men. Rather than encouraging them to continue struggling, lesbians can support their breaking free from such relationships. We can, from a position of power as strong women, talk with other women about their relationships with men while at the same time making it clear that our primary concern is for the well being of the woman and not necessarily the preservation of the relationship.

Lesbian and heterosexual women working together

Lesbians and heterosexual women have always worked together, though the non-lesbian women haven't always known it. Where there are women's centers, women's bookstores, women's counseling services, battered women's shelters, there are lesbians. Where there are struggles for day care, job equality, women's rights legislation, and even abortion and birth control, there are lesbians. Where there are girls' camps, women's schools, women's organizations, there are lesbians. Inside and outside the political movement, women's space draws lesbians for work and play, because that is where many of us feel most comfortable and committed.

Women's political work—the suffrage movement, abolition, organizing of women workers, and today's women's movement—has always had a large share of lesbians, often in leadership positions. But it is only recently that lesbians have become vocal and visible both in our separate organizations (Daughters of Bilitis, Radicalesbians, National Lesbian Feminist Organization) and in broader-based groups like the National Organization for Women and women's caucuses in political parties and in left organizations.

The result has often been bitter fighting between lesbians and non-lesbians. Some women's organizations have wanted to keep lesbians out (of the organizations and the movement) because they feared society as a whole would reject the women's movement totally if lesbians were associated with it. Keeping women in line through fear of being called lesbians, with the oppressive treatment that follows, is called "lesbian-baiting," and it has been very effective both in keeping lesbian and heterosexual women at each other's throats (and thus weakening them politically) and in holding heterosexual women back from taking the most radical stands.

As a matter of fact, lesbian presence in the women's movement has had a positive influence by:

—pushing women who identify as heterosexual to commit more energy to women

—presenting a radical alternative in lifestyle and political perspective which makes it easier for some women to move in that direction

—insisting that women explore the basic reasons for women's oppression and acknowledge that society must change in radical ways to stop it

NO TURNING BACK: LESBIAN AND GAY
LIBERATION FOR THE 80'S, Goodman, Lakey, Lashof, and Thorne

name   address   phone

—encouraging the women's movement to look at class, race, age, and religious oppression among women.

The traditional lesbian separatist vision of a world in which women are superior, even though it is a minority viewpoint and not one with which we agree, has been a catalyst for other women to develop more radical visions of their own.

Though the wounds from this battle are deep, and many are still unhealed, we see hopeful signs that women are beginning to work together more effectively:

—Lesbian presence is much more an expected, if not fully accepted, part of women working together.

—Lesbian caucuses are now common in women's organizations and functions, helping to give individual lesbians both support and power in the larger groups.

—The concept, existence, and shape of lesbianism has received a fair amount of media attention, thus speeding society's acknowledgement of our culture.

—There is a spirit of openness on both sides, hard to define but possible to perceive all over the country, to working together with common values and goals. An example of this spirit is the "Take Back the Night" movement, which is active in most large cities. Take Back the Night marches and rallies have attracted phenomenal numbers of women (10,000 in New York, 4,300 in Minneapolis, 6,000 in Philadelphia). Many Take Back the Night groups have a core of lesbians, and a lesbian-feminist analysis is used to explain violence against women and how to stop it. But the marches and rallies themselves attract all women and cut across class, race, and age lines in the issues they address.

These actions have infused the women's and lesbian political atmosphere in many areas of the country with new life and are models of cooperative work.

We sense that this fresh energy that lesbian and non-lesbian women have for working together will continue and grow. We feel that a crucial next step in the lesbian and gay liberation movement is to recognize what lesbians and non-lesbians share and how we can act out of our unity instead of our divisions.

As lesbians reach out to non-lesbians in political work, we must of course be prepared to recognize situations in which we are treated as less than full, important partners and decide either to confront these situations and continue the cooperative effort, or to stop because the cost is too great. But we *can* put aside the pain of past fighting to develop methods of organizing which allow all the women involved to be freely themselves and proud of their identity.

Feminist and non-feminist women

Although a line can sometimes be usefully drawn between women who are still primarily "agents of the oppressor" and women who are not, it cannot be drawn according to a woman's sexual identity. The real difference is between woman-identified women—those who are serious about feminist struggle and loving women—and women who are still allied mainly with men; and there are heterosexual, bisexual and homosexual women on both sides.

All women have been socialized to accept our own situations as natural and even desirable and to reinforce sexism in others. So thorough has the training been that most non-feminist women will furiously defend their position against any who challenge it. This is painful and difficult for any feminist, yet non-feminist women need to be confronted and not avoided if all women are to gain the consciousness needed to fight patriarchal oppression. Women who are feminists cannot afford to abandon those who are still clinging to the belief that they are not oppressed. Moreover, it is not fair to those women to leave them in a place where all feminists were once. This is true for all feminists, gay or non-gay, with regard to all non-feminists, gay or non-gay.

Feminists relating to non-feminists need to remember that the actual woman underneath the conditioning is a sister, and that despite her assertions to the contrary she is hurting from patriarchal treatment. Feminists need to find creative ways of reaching for that human being, making connections with her as a person and pointing up common concerns and needs. We can begin gently to interrupt her sexism, explaining how it belittles women and causes us suffering, and how things might be different.

At the same time, it is essential never to put a woman down for her lack of feminist consciousness. She is not to blame for her socially instilled behavior patterns, nor for the fact that she has been deceived into thinking she is free. Feminists need to remember that many women are scared and alienated by the feminist movement and that the way to reach them will never be through attacking or blaming them, but through appreciating and caring for them, combined with gentle challenging. If we are correct that women are indeed oppressed, such women will naturally want to seek liberation, and to fight for it, once they are aware that they have been held down. It is useless and damaging to try to force or guilt-trip a woman into feminist consciousness.

Feminists must also recognize that fear, pain, misinformation (or no information) and a lack of perceived alternatives are the real obstacles preventing a woman from becoming a feminist. We must relate to her with much patience and sensitivity as well as loving support. We must start at her level and move forward with her at her pace, appreciating that she is doing the best she can in her situation. We should never give up on her, even though it may be a slow and frustrating process.

At the same time, feminists need to recognize the limitations of our energy, make commitments only when it makes sense, and not feel responsible for changing every woman's consciousness overnight. After all, it's a big job.

Lesbian mothers with male children

It is important that lesbian mothers with male children not be isolated, excluded, or made to feel guilty by other lesbians because they maintain their love for and commitments to their children. Lesbian mothers with male children should not be isolated in their homes any more than wives should be, and since, as lesbians, they are unlikely to receive much support from heterosexual people or organizations, it is all the more important that the gay community assume responsibility for helping them raise their children. This means men as well as women. Gay people concerned about helping to free our sisters will want to assist a lesbian mother in her child-raising duties.

However, lesbian mothers must respect the fact that women have a legitimate need for womanspace and a safe haven from sexism. Socialization of male children begins early—in fact, as soon as a boy begins to have contact with the outside world. It is impossible for a boy to totally escape sexist conditioning. Thus there will be women-only occasions to which it is not appropriate for a lesbian to bring her male child. She should not, however, be excluded because of her child. We recommend that organizers of such events enlist a man or men to do childcare for the male children in another place. This is not only a way to meet the needs of mothers with boys, it is also a way for men to (re)learn how to play, to relate to children and to be affectionate, assertively gentle male models. It is, therefore, important to the men's own development as well as to the children's.

Lesbian separatists do have a right to be with just women, and to exclude even young male children too, if that is important to them. However, this is a personal need for womanspace and not a political statement, and it should be viewed as such. Obviously, separatist women who want a lesbian nation will disagree with this. Since excluding male children will inevitably exclude some lesbian mothers some of the time, we should avoid making such a demand if it is not necessary.

All adults, including lesbians and gay men, need to pay attention to childcare. Where possible, childcare should be arranged for all women's events, since otherwise many mothers, non-gay, gay, and potentially gay, will be excluded. Perhaps the women at the event can share the care of the female children collectively, while men care for the male children elsewhere.

Lesbians and gay men without children need to think about making a commitment to children's liberation and about the best kind of relationships to have with young people. We should not consider ourselves automatically absolved of all responsibility to children just because we do not have any of our own. In addition to organizing childcare at women's events, we particularly encourage gay men to make ongoing commitments to male children. This is an excellent opportunity to free mothers from the burden of constant childcare while showing young boys an anti-sexist male model. It is particularly appropriate for gay men (and heterosexual men with no children) to spend time with the male children of lesbians—that is, boys who might otherwise have no men in their lives. Most lesbians are faced with the dilemma of either isolating a boy from other men or of exposing him to men who will teach him to be more sexist. All boys need non-sexist men to relate to.

Lesbians must be careful not to dump their anger at adult sexist men onto boy children. When a boy behaves in a sexist fashion, we should put aside our feeling that we cannot change men and that it is not worth the energy to try. This is simply not accurate when dealing with boy children because women do have the power to change a child's behavior and to raise boys to be nurturing adults. When a sexist incident occurs, we can explain to both female and male children what is happening and why it is hurtful to women. Moreover, women should be aware of our own conditioned feelings of hopelessness and powerlessness and avoid transmitting them to our children. Boys should not be allowed to believe that, no matter what they do, they will become sexist monsters, nor girls led to expect to be unable to do anything about sexist incidents.

We should all recognize the need to raise male children in such a way that they do not grow up to be oppressors of women, and we should respect women as well as men who choose to put energy into doing this. Such energy is not wasted, nor diverted from the feminist struggle, if we can raise boys so that they can be nurturing, non-oppressive adults. However, women who choose to live or work with male children also must realize that it is not possible to raise a totally non-sexist boy in this society at this time.

For lesbians living collectively, it makes sense for those who are not threatened by living with male children to include boys in their households and for those who need space from *all* males, including young boys, to live separately. In making these decisions, we should be sensitive to the needs of mothers for lesbian support. We should not make the mistake of thinking that it is "purer" or "politically correct" to abandon lesbian mothers and male children to isolation.

Many women are forced to live with men because they cannot survive economically on their own, especially if they have or want children. Such women are not usually able to act on their feelings for other women, either sexually or politically. Lesbians without children or other dependents can use their relatively greater earning power to help give these women other choices, by offering to share income, communal houses, and childcare responsibilities with them. As such options become more widespread and better known, more and more women will be free to choose whether they want to continue relating to men sexually and socially or whether they prefer relationships with other women. Lesbians need to consider our responsibilities to all children, not just those children whose mothers already define themselves as lesbians.

Separatism and men

All but the most extreme separatist lesbians have a few personal connections with men, a few males whom we love and care about. These men are often our close relatives or others whom we have loved deeply over a period of time. There is nothing un-radical or un-feminist about a woman who is committed to women but who maintains loving relationships with those few men in the world whom she finds herself still able to love despite their sexist training. Indeed, as we have said, it is important for women separatists to keep in touch with the reality that men can be beautiful, loving human beings underneath their sexist behavior.

When I first came out, I felt very guilty about continuing to feel love for Paul, the man I had been lovers with. I was ashamed to have other lesbians know, fearing they would think I was not a "proper" lesbian or that it was "politically incorrect" to feel any affection for any man. It took me a while to figure out my own politics and to stop feeling so uncomfortable. Now I am delighted that the relationship we built while we were lovers was strong enough to survive all the pain and the changes and to transform itself into a very special friendship.

Of course men do change when women struggle with them individually, especially those men committed to personal growth and human liberation. But one woman struggling with one man does so in isolation and weakness. Men will listen and change much faster when women are united and powerful. One-to-one struggling *is* valid, but it is not the most effective use of feminist energy, and if adopted as the primary way to fight sexism, it is likely to fail. We need an army of women on the streets to go around saying, "You men won't do this any more." Men will take feminists seriously when we women put our sisters and our liberation struggle first, when we have built real power and can say to men, "We don't need you for anything any more."

The reasons why separatism is especially important for women as an oppressed group are the very reasons why it is particularly threatening to men. Because most men, unlike other oppressors, have close relationships with individual members of the group they dominate, they are affected personally when women become separatists. Much of men's self-image depends on women "needing" them; thus when women withdraw, men lose more than the nurturing and emotional support they are accustomed to. Their sense of themselves and of their role in the world is also radically challenged. Women's separatism is very hard for men to accept, even if they appreciate the need for it intellectually: they need and deserve much support from their brothers in dealing with their feelings about it.

Men learning to love and care for each other is a vital part of the struggle against patriarchy, as we have shown. We want men to work against their training to be cool, tough, unemotional, defensive, and competitive toward other men, and their training to be emotionally dependent on women, a dependency that absorbs women's energies. As more and more women claim our right to womanspace *and* refuse to listen to men's feelings about our doing so, more and more men will be motivated to unlearn this training. Thus a side effect of women's separatism is to stimulate major emotional growth for men.

Men will probably not be able to identify and root out all their sexist training by themselves, however, since behavior that feels oppressive to women may be accepted by other men as natural and normal, all men having been trained to behave that way. At some point, therefore, men will need the help of women to give up their remaining sexist behavior. But men can go a long way by challenging, loving, and supporting each other; we insist that they combat as much of their sexism on their own as they can, so as to leave women the space and energy to organize our own struggle.

Women's separatism feels terrible to men. Men's feelings about it often go something like this: "It's not fair. I don't want to be sexist. I didn't choose to be raised that way and I'm trying hard to break out of it. I also feel very guilty about the ways I have been oppressive when I didn't mean to; they weren't my fault, either. Why are you women deserting me when I'm trying so hard? I'm really on your side, you know." There is an element of truth to these reactions. Women's enemy is the system of patriarchy, not individual men. We know that men did not choose to be sexist and do not blame them for their socialization as males. At the same time, we do insist that men take responsibility for stepping out of their sexism. The most effective thing anti-sexist men can do at this time is to take responsibility for each other, thus avoiding demanding women's energy and attention. Doing this may feel to men as if they are being condemned and abandoned by women, rather than taking an active, positive part in the feminist struggle; but it is important to remember that this is truly the best way forward to our goal of a society in which we can all be loving and peaceful with each other. The feelings of rejection deserve attention *as feelings*, but they should not be mistaken for political thinking.

Our conclusion is that men can greatly aid the feminist struggle by giving women support to be separate, and especially by learning to support and care for each other.

Chapter VI

Gay Men: Culture and Strategy

In this section, as in Lesbian Culture and Strategy, we first focus on the specific gay experience, including what is positive about our culture and what needs to be improved; then we look at ways men can take responsibility for changing ourselves* and thus affect the entire society.

Gay Men's Culture

The visible gay scene is only the tip of the iceberg of gay sexuality in this country. There are many gay men who do not participate in the "gay world" of parties, bars, community centers, churches, conferences, baths, and civil rights groups. Alfred Kinsey's famous study of male sexuality found that over one-third of the men in his sample acknowledged having experienced sex with another man, including orgasm, *after* puberty. But many of those men never become comfortable with that part of their sexuality. They do not seek support for it by associating with other gay men.

Probably ten percent of the male population is consciously gay for a considerable period of their lives, but even many of these men do not participate in the gay social world, a world that is much smaller than the perhaps 10 million gay men in America.

The gay men's culture is, however, extremely important for a study of gay liberation, because it is the main social space from which gay work for change occurs. When a fund-raising affair is organized to support the fight for gay rights, for example, activists canvas the gay bars to sell tickets. When a new gay newspaper is launched, introductory copies are circulated in the places where gay men gather. The newspaper may find its way eventually into the hands of many gay men who do not "make the gay scene," but the paper generally needs the core of support found in the bars and other gathering places in order to survive and grow.

This writing reflects who we, the authors, are: urban and white. We are not able to write about the experience of gay men of color nor of rural gays, who have their own unique situations.[1]

---

*In this section gay men, and sometimes all men, are "we."

Vitality of the gay world

The (male) gay world is an oasis in the desert of mainstream society; many of us have reached it thirsty, and rejoiced when we found it.[2] It has vitality and creativity. For those of us who are gay, it functions in several important ways:

—providing personal support in securing a firm sense of self
—offering a place to find friends and lovers
—presenting more accurate information about gay oppression than we can get in the heterosexual world
—teaching skills, all the way from sex to vocations
—providing an environment for working for change politically
—being a seedbed for cultural change.

The gay world is a place where we can come to terms with gayness in our image of ourselves. Even in the grim '50s, a measure of self-acceptance could be gained there. In the documentary film *Word Is Out*, a man named George describes getting to know gay life in San Francisco:

. . . And so that year I began to get oriented to the gay community, and I used to go to the Black Cat every Sunday afternoon. This was about 1952 or 1953, somewhere in there. I found out that they had a satirical opera done in a comical way on Sundays. They had an entertainer named Jose, and he used to put on crazy women's hats and do *Carmen*—using these crazy outfits, and he had a pianist who'd play. . . . And then he would do Carmen with this crazy hat, dancing around the stage trying to hide from the vice squad who were in the bushes trying to capture Carmen. The best thing was that he did it very deliberately, with a spirit of unity. There used to be maybe two hundred people would fill this bar, and they would all cheer this satire, which was basically the beginning of gay liberation. . . .

You must realize that the vice squad was there. At that time they used to park their police cars outside of gay bars, and they used to take down the names of people when they entered. They used to come in and stand around and just generally intimidate people and make them feel that they were less than human. It was a frightening period. I am very stirred by this, because at that time there was no place to go for your freedom, and you were very much aware that there was no freedom and that your freedom was in a gay bar, and when you got out on the streets you were Mr. Straight or Miss Straight.[3]

Martin Weinberg and Colin Williams did a landmark study of gay men in the late '60s and early '70s called *Male Homosexuals*. In their interviews they asked how involved the men were with other gays, and how they were coping with life in general. They found that the men who did not associate much with other gays experienced more depression, and also guilt, shame, or anxiety about their gayness; they were more likely to want psychiatric treatment.[4]

The gay world is also a place to find friends and lovers. Heterosexuals find it easier to find mates in the natural course of work or recreation because most people identify as heterosexual; striking up a potentially sexual friendship with someone you meet while bowling is easier if you are heterosexual than if you are gay. Many gays can tell heartbreaking stories of people they fell in love with who turned out not to be gay and broke off the friendship when sexual interest was expressed. It is important, therefore, to have a place to go where the friends you make will not reject you because of your gayness.

The gay world also provides information on gay oppression which gives a broader basis for generalizations than does an individual's own personal experience. There he will hear horror stories and also stories of decency. Most important, he will learn that survival, despite the oppression, is commonplace! In their interviews, Weinberg and Williams found that the men who were least involved with other gays exaggerated the danger and expected more hassle from the heterosexual world than did gays who were more involved with other gays.[5]

Skills can be picked up in the gay world, for there are many men who assume they should be "big brothers" and show newcomers the ropes. Any gay lifestyle involves a number of skills: the best way to come out to parents, how to handle the landlord, and so on. Even sexual activities are learned in the gay world: since, in this society, there is severe disapproval of some common gay sexual techniques, newcomers to gayness are often inhibited and need patient teaching to become skillful in sharing sexual satisfaction.[6]

The gay world provides a place to mobilize for action against gay oppression. Gay liberation requires, most of all, that gays take the lead in making changes. Though substantial changes cannot happen without alliances with non-gays, gays themselves must take the initiative. That requires enough acceptance of self and trust in others to provide a basis for cohesion. The gay world is where self-acceptance and mutual trust grow. We believe that the gay men's culture can become much more supportive of liberation than it is now; there are many problems in the gay men's culture. We will suggest some changes, but our suggestions are made against the background of appreciation for the oasis which the gay world has been in a desert of gay oppression.

The gay world is also a seedbed for cultural change; its creativity often spills over into mainstream society. A current example is disco. In just a few years the disco beat has spread from gay bars into the neighborhood skating rinks and popular radio stations. John Travolta, in the film *Saturday Night Fever*, is seen by many as a masculine figure, yet his dance floor performance is so gay that he would have been beaten up for acting like that in a '50s high school dance. The mainstream culture has changed to give permission (on a disco floor) for heterosexually identified men to be as flashy, as extravagant in gesture, as free in body as gay men have often allowed ourselves to be. This is a long way from the gray flannel suit and the modest fox-trot which once typified the restrained fun of middle-class America. As is often the case in cultural trends, some celebrity-upper-class people picked up and adopted the looseness some working-class people had begun discovering. The celebrities made it respectable for trendy middle-class young people to try. Disco is *loud* (and so, even in the gay world, working-class gays probably took to it more quickly than dignified middle-class gays). Dancing to disco is like having a fling; until you are used to it you feel slightly outrageous, and, as dance forms go, there is tremendous room for individual variation. Disco is sensual and even sexual; again, as in the men's world, sex is right out front. Disco is a chance to do dress-up, which many boys missed out on while the girls were raiding grandmother's trunk.

We are not saying that disco is the ultimate as a form of celebration. Nor have we failed to notice the wooden faces that sometimes appear on the disco floor. Compared, however, to traditional styles of heterosexual dance, disco offers a new opportunity for the release of our whole selves in the context of popular dancing.

The dress-up, the wider range of gestures, and the outrageous boisterousness of disco connect it to camp, an earlier (and more elaborate) art form which was born among gays and adopted by some in the heterosexual world. Camp is a particular way of making fun; gays refer to "camping it up." It is a combination of conversation and role-play in which the wit turns on the absurdity of sex role conventions. It springs from the experience of gays who grew up knowing that the world is different from the official interpretation of reality given by adults. By extension, camp art objects are those which are out of place; camp becomes a light-hearted embrace of the incongruous.[7]

We could give other examples of cultural inventions originating in the gay world and nurtured there until the broader culture was ready to use them. The Bloomsbury group of leading intellectuals in England in the early part of this century, for example, has received little attention for its fostering of the idea of androgyny. Writer Virginia Woolf and economist John Maynard Keynes were two well-known members of that group, which supported its members' strivings for androgyny—and gayness—while on the margin of proper English society.

The vitality of the gay men's culture is expressed in the many ways it supports gay consciousness and lifestyle: affirming identity, providing information about oppression, sharing skills, helping friends and lovers find each other, providing support in political mobilization, and encouraging cultural change. Its importance may be taken for granted at a time when it is not so costly for some men to discover their gayness, yet this excerpt from a letter reveals the value of the gay support group which the writer had just begun:

Funny—when I first came out 8 years ago, I felt, "What's all this oppression stuff? I'm gay, big deal." (I had not *consciously* repressed gayness in my younger years.) Now I'm a furious man. The insidious, subtle pressures I've swayed with these past years, the fact that there has been so little encouragement in thirty years to *delight* in my sexuality, period, let alone sexual preferences. . . .

Even a man who thought he didn't need support ("I'm gay, big deal") has found the subtle ways in which he was made numb by the pervasiveness of gay oppression. He, like the rest of us, needs the support of other gays.

Decadence

It is not only Christians and other religious fundamentalists who worry about gay men's culture. Communists, fascists, and other political sorts have all attacked the gay men's culture as "decadent"—unwholesome weird sensuality for its own sake, preoccupation with what "feels good," glorification of pleasure without commitment or the context of community. Some gays have responded to these criticisms by embracing the virtures of bourgeois respectability: church-going, monogamous gay marriages, high status careers, refined tastes.

Historically, gays have had to live their gayness in the cracks of society, where the other outcasts are.

Sometimes my work takes me to strange cities where I have to work under a lot of pressure. If I can manage it I like to wander to the part of downtown where the prostitutes and hustlers and street people hang out and the gay bars are. There I know I'll be accepted for who I am, not for the work I do, or what I can do for people. We all have our quirks and hang-ups. In that part of town I know I won't find people judging me.

Younger gays who have come out since 1969 and the advent of the gay liberation movement have a hard time appreciating older gay men's experience of expressing their gayness in the cracks of society. But this experience affected the world view of men who came out before 1969 in several ways. (These are, of course, generalizations and do not fit every person):

—some sympathy for the position of outcasts in general, the marginal ones
—a feeling of unworthiness because of associating with "the dregs of society"
—an attachment by some to capitalist society because capitalism, being more loosely organized than socialist societies generally are,

has more cracks for gays to fit into (for example, Batista's Cuba
compared with Castro's Cuba)
—a higher degree of tolerance for others; a reluctance to put down
the behavior of others.

One of the hardest tasks of gay liberation is to sort out what is positive
and what is negative in our experience. It is analogous to the Black
experience. Blacks did not choose slavery and the years of oppression that
have followed. Yet, out of that degrading situation a culture developed
which is contributing to the liberation of all humans. That is the way of
the human spirit: in the midst of hardship, new and positive things can
emerge. But Blacks have needed to sort through that cultural heritage.
They have had to discard the things which once helped them adapt to
the oppressive situation but which later became obstacles to liberation,
like the shuffling pose adopted in front of white people.

Gays must also do some sifting out. We are mistaken when we agree
whole-heartedly with our critics and disavow gay men's culture as worthless
and then try to mimic heterosexual respectability. We are also mistaken
when we try to defend every practice and every confusion that we find
among gay men. Gay liberation, when fully realized, will mean no longer
living in the cracks, because society will have changed fundamentally and
will have incorporated some aspects of gay culture into itself.

Let's look, for example, at the baths, or "the tubs" as they are also called.
A gay bath typically has a steam room, showers, a lounge with magazines
and refreshments, a whirlpool tub, rows of tiny rooms with a bed in each,
and an "orgy room"—a darkened room with a huge bedspace and perhaps
smaller beds. The club may also have a disco floor, a swimming pool, an
exercise room, cabaret/theater space, and other facilities. The members
of the club generally walk around wearing towels around their waists,
seeking out sexual partners. Sex takes place in the tiny bedrooms, the orgy
room, almost everywhere.

Gay men who dislike the baths deplore the anonymous character of the
sex, the risk of transmitting VD, the ease of sexual objectification. The
baths seem, despite the availability of soap and water, the incarnation of
"dirtiness."

Many members of baths deliberately choose anonymity because they
have jobs or marriages which would be threatened by the exposure of their
gayness. Police seem to know this: each year we hear of police raids on
the baths in several cities, a terrifying experience to men who have a lot
to lose by coming out.

What is positive about the baths?

—Friendships are born there. Contrary to popular impression, men
do sometimes make lasting friendships with people they meet at the
baths.

—There is permission for free sexuality, in which the play element
of sex becomes intensified by the absence of relationship worries.

What I see at the baths is like a children's playground. Someone is standing by the see-saw and I join him to see-saw for awhile, then go off to the swings until I feel like joining a few others at the sandbox. I play and play, now with one, then with several, and alone when I feel like being alone. Like the children at the playground, I don't need to know names or the histories of their lives to have a good time.

—Caring and tenderness is expressed. The idea that caring is restricted to people you know is mistaken, as anyone who has comforted a stranger at the scene of an accident can tell you.

—It is a space for experimenting with new approaches to sex.

I decided I was ready to try something that was very scary for me: to be completely passive and just receive pleasure. So I lay on a bed in the orgy room and waited in the darkness, shivering as I lay there. Someone approached who stroked too roughly: I motioned him away. Another touched me gently and I let him stay; he was soon joined by someone else who was smooth and electric at the same time. I forced myself to lie there passively instead of reciprocating their caresses, and was pleasured for the longest time, trembling with fear and catching images of what the fear was about even as my body responded with warmth and delight.

Like all of today's institutions, the baths are an amalgam of good and bad elements. People get stuck there, locked in sexual rituals that prevent them from being truly and humanly vulnerable—or they can use the chance to grow and share. What we can be proud of in the baths are the elements that we will seek in the new society: friendship and caring, delight in sexual play, and an experimental approach to sexuality.

Getting it together: problems in the gay men's culture

We gays are the ones who need to change our community and remove the blocks that get in our way when we seek to love each other and to work for liberation. Six blocks seem especially prominent: racism, classism, ageism, chemical dependency, sexism, and violence. All of these are rampant in the mainstream culture, of course, and they help to account for why so many heterosexual people are hurting. But it is our special responsibility to clean up our own act as gays; that means taking a critical look at what happens among us.

Racism: Racist discrimination is still a fact of life in the gay world. There are bars that are all-white or nearly so and baths that discriminate. Gay rights organizations often content themselves with mere token participation by Third World people. Gays of color have to deal with racist attitudes that range from blatant to subtle. Some white gays, for example, see only the color in another gay man and expect him at every moment to be representing his culture. That is tedious and degrading; individuals need to be appreciated for their whole selves, not just one part. Other whites pretend to be color-blind, and act as if the man is neutral (which generally works out in practice to be white). Color-blindness overlooks a dimension of the man which is extremely important to his sense of self and to his experience. It is like those friends of gays who never refer to gayness or to gay issues; they render their gay friends invisible even though the gays are open with them, because they refuse to see clearly the person they call their friend.

Men of color can relax in a mixed group only if their white friends relax; they can feel that they are recognized only if their friends are genuinely interested in their whole lives, including their color. As long as white men are shy or hold back for fear of making mistakes, they will perpetuate tension and misunderstanding.

There is probably less racism in the gay world than in the heterosexual world, since there is little family pressure in determining who one's lover will be. The family influence which restrains heterosexual Jews from dating non-Jews, Catholics from dating Protestants, upper-class people from dating working-class people, and whites from dating Blacks is largely removed from the decisions of gay men. Gays are, therefore, more free to love people who are different from themselves. However, gays have been conditioned in a racist society just as heterosexuals have, and the deep-grained prejudices must be worked through.

Classism: Classism messes us up both politically and personally. Politically, we get confused by classism so we do not see that the most influential group in society is the owning class; we don't see how small that group is, and how its power must be redistributed if we are to have a really democratic society with fair decision making. Personally, gay men get involved in status and snobbery games which waste energy and result in a lot of people feeling bad about themselves. Gay men miss out on a lot of the love and sharing that is potentially there for them because they respond to class, rather than human, signals. They shun those they consider beneath them, and are intimidated by those they imagine to be superior in terms of wealth, education, and culture.

I often start to feel bad and drop out of the conversation when it turns to something like European travel. Men talk about their wild gay adventures in various European cities or about which places they liked best and I feel uncomfortable. I know I never had the chance to do those things—for me, deep-sea fishing 50 miles from home was a big deal—and my friends probably wouldn't be interested in my stories about that.

This sense of inferiority is reinforced when the working-class gay man notices that the spokespeople for gay men's movements are almost always middle or upper-middle class.

The gay world offers an avenue of upward mobility for some bright and attractive working-class men. It often happens that a working-class youth will become the lover of a middle/upper class-man and will then learn the ways and attitudes of the dominant classes. He is introduced to gourmet cooking and the pleasures of the ballet, but his own background remains unexplored and unappreciated by the circle he is moving in, and he learns to ignore and even put down his own "vulgar" origins. Instead of changing the attitudes in the middle- or upper-middle-class portion of the class-divided gay male movement, he becomes co-opted into it.

Ageism: Ageism is another system of attitudes which prevents unity in the gay male world. It assigns values to people according to the generation they belong to. In its estimation of sexual attractiveness, the gay culture mimics the mainstream culture by glorifying youth and regarding older men as undesirable. In the gay men's culture, sexual attractiveness is a larger part of the organizing dynamic of life and ageism is probably more pronounced even than in the mainstream.

We older gay men are looked upon as inferior in appearance, attractiveness, intelligence and sexual prowess. Many of us have unwittingly accepted our alleged inferiority. Consequently, we cannot relate to other gay men our age—we must pursue the eternal 18-year-old Adonis. . . . And why is it that when an older gay man cruises he is dirty?[8]

This attitude hurts everyone. The various age groups have a lot to share with each other and the movement needs the gifts of each generation. The stereotype of older gay men as lonely and sad individuals is untrue. Weinberg and Williams found in their interview study of 2400 gay men, *Male Homosexuals*, that there were "no age-related differences in self-acceptance, anxiety, depression, or loneliness. In fact, our data suggest that in some respects our older homosexuals have greater well-being than our younger homosexuals."[9]

Relationships across generational lines can be unusually rich *because* of the differences: each person anchored in different formative influences, the older person often bringing experience, broader contacts, more self-knowledge, more ability to nurture his partner and the relationship, while the younger person often brings fresh enthusiasm, the experience of having been reared in a sexually freer environment, a clearer need to be nurtured, and an easy acceptance of the older man's caring. Such differences as these, especially when acknowledged and valued, can add to a friendship which is developing out of common interests and mutual attraction.

Ageism turns generational differences into hassles instead of sources of enrichment.

Bob and I have been lovers for nearly two years. I am in my early twenties and he is twice my age. Since we first became friends I have had to fight off the feeling that "there must be something weird about this. He's too old and I'm too young for us really to be friends." Besides coming to the relationship with that idea, I've also gotten the same message from friends of ours.

Something which complicates it all is having been treated badly by a high school teacher of mine (partly because of my age) and then assuming that because of similarities of age and appearance between him and Bob, that Bob would treat me the same.

Another variation of ageism, sometimes called adultism, is looking down on young people and refusing to take them seriously as partners in the struggle for gay liberation, or even as persons. Stereotypes such as "flighty," "naive," "cute but ineffectual" take power and influence away from youths. Some older gay men that call young men, "sweet young things," just as some heterosexual men call women.

As in the struggles against racism and classism in the gay male world, the goal we seek is for each male to be treated with respect as the unique person he is, taking all his characteristics into account, not for the purpose of exploitation or stereotyping, but to know him better as a whole human being. We must fight society's denial of power to young people, which is frequently rationalized as being "in their best interest." Some of the gay movements in Europe, for example, have been successfully campaigning to lower the age of consent for sexual activity. Through lobbying as well as through support for gay youth groups, adult gays in this country can learn how to be non-paternalistic allies of younger gays.

Chemical dependency: Because so much of our social life and personal support has historically been centered on the bar scene, gay men often have a problem with dependence on alcohol and other drugs. In this way, gay men are also related to mainstream society, of course, where alcoholism is on the increase and people depend on caffeine, nicotine, and pep pills to keep running in the rat-race; and marijuana, cocaine, tranquilizers and other drugs to get some release from it. What we want to do is to eliminate the rat-race and create the kind of society that we deserve. But many give in to hopelessness, and give up power to chemicals. It is significant that many movements for national liberation, such as the Front for National Liberation in Algeria and the Indian National Congress in India, have struggled against drug abuse at the same time they have struggled against imperial domination. They needed people to take back the power they had given to drugs so they would have the ability and energy to take back the power relinquished to empires.

Violence: It is only reasonable for us to want to be powerful—to take charge of our lives, to set goals and achieve them, to be able to influence others when we have clarity in a certain area. Unfortunately, the patriarchal culture has added to our reasonable need for power an unreasonable desire: to dominate others and control them. The system gives us, as men, a dominant position over women and children and tells us that we cannot feel good about ourselves as men unless we exploit that position. When male domination is challenged, the threat or use of physical violence is the traditional male response.

Violence in mainstream culture, therefore, is a masculine preoccupation. It starts for us as boys when we have to face the schoolyard bully and deal with the pecking order that develops on the basis of who can beat up whom. Many gay men intuitively knew as boys that this whole game was nonsense and somehow bound up with oppression; often we bailed out and were called "sissies."

The intuition that violence is oppressive seemed to be present in gay liberation organizations as they arose in the '70s; many committed themselves to nonviolent action in their by-laws, though their members often had little exposure to the ideology and strategies of nonviolence.

In conflict with our intuitive search for non-patriarchal ways of waging our struggle is the broad assumption in patriarchal culture that "when you get serious about power you need violence." After years of struggling nonviolently for change, gay men may be attracted to violence in much the same way as Blacks were in the mid-60s, and with similar harmful effects on the momentum of the movement. To prevent this from happening, we think it is time for gay men to study seriously the means of nonviolent struggle. We need to study not only our own experience of the last decade but also to learn from other struggles against oppression. The Harvard scholar Dr. Gene Sharp, in his book *The Politics of Nonviolent Action*, describes 198 methods of nonviolent struggle which have so far been used by various movements for justice.[10] Another good point of departure for thinking about these issues is the chapter "Why Not Armed Struggle?" in *Moving Toward a New Society*.

The patriarchal culture goes one step beyond connecting power with domination and violence: it connects both with sexuality. In the mainstream this is seen most clearly in rape, an act of violence expressed through sexual contact. Rape is a way of subduing; it is an extreme of the playboy's dream of conquest. Rape occurs on a large scale when an army invades another country, as Susan Brownmiller reports in *Against Our Will*, because it is another way of asserting dominance.[11]

We naturally must ask whether this patriarchal equation of power/domination/violence/sex has crept into the gay men's culture through the practice of sado-masochism. At first glance it looks to some people as though S&M is simply sexual violence. The issue is more complicated than that, however, because S&M partners are using pain voluntarily; unlike rape, S&M is not usually a matter of coercion. Participants in S&M may experience themselves as involved primarily with mutuality, with trust, and with sensuality.[12]

Further, we need to tread carefully because S&M lends itself to the focus of renewed homophobic attacks on gayness itself. Films like *Cruising* that sensationalize the leather-bar scene can fuel oppression especially if we divide ourselves politically between those who do and those who don't engage in S&M.

Taking all this into account, the authors of this book consider it right to challenge the value of S&M. The symbolism is pretty clear: motorcycles, chains, and leather as badges of sexiness suggest to us that S&M is in fact an expression of the patriarchal connection of masculine power/domination with sexuality. (This is not to say, of course, that owning a motorcycle means participating in S&M!) Even though it is voluntary, the sexual acting out of domination-submission accompanied by the infliction of pain seems to us an intimate re-run of the daily oppression experienced in a patriarchal society. The fact that there is pleasure in it is no more relevant than the fact that there is pleasure in chemical dependency.

We realize that this is an emotional subject for many people, and we are not trying to condemn anyone whose sexuality has become linked to the broader oppression of violence. Some men who are exploring S&M may be working through, in a safe context (with someone they trust and care about), the psychological areas where they got stuck as youngsters. The question for us as individuals on violence, as with classism or racism or any other oppression which affects us, is not, Where am I right now? but, In what direction am I heading? We need not waste energy on guilt or in putting ourselves down for ways we have been caught by the negativities in our culture. Far better to realize the many ways we have done well, and to reach out for support for further growth.

Sexism: Many women would rather associate with gay men than with heterosexual men because they often experience less sexism from gay men. Nevertheless, the patriarchy has bent the minds of gay men in many ways. Gay men have, after all, been brought up to be masculine in this society and have absorbed some of its anti-woman prejudice. The intimate connection between gay liberation and the feminist struggle requires that we sort this out very carefully.

There are woman-hating gay men; it is not surprising that people who have been hurt themselves sometimes lash out at others who seem vulnerable and are said by society to be beneath them. Further, many gay men have been in situations where they had to pretend to erotic feelings for women when they really preferred men; this may have spurred feelings of hostility toward the group of people for whom they feigned affection.

Gay male activists as a whole are not woman-haters, yet there is a traditional sexist domination of the lesbian and gay rights movement by men. Women rarely act as representatives of a mixed gay group. When most Americans think "gay," they think "men." It is difficult for lesbians to get media coverage because of this distorted image with which many gay male activists cooperate. At mixed-sex meetings, women are more often interrupted and less carefully listened to. The reasons why separate womanspace is needed are often dismissed.

Changes are under way. The 1979 march in Washington for lesbian and gay rights reflected a substantial change from even a few years earlier:

lesbian culture was the tone-setter of the stage presentations, women played visible roles at all levels, feminism was generally assumed as a frame of reference.

At the rally in Washington I was standing next to a group of lesbians. I enjoyed their pleasure as well as my own when women like Meg Christian made their presentations. But then when Holly Near sang "Somewhere Over the Rainbow" tears trickled down my cheeks. It took me a minute to realize why: this one had special meaning for us older gay men.

Even though changes are occurring, much more needs to be done to root out the effects of sexism on gay men. The most persistent problem is men's unwillingness to really understand how patriarchy works. Gay oppression is part of the system of patriarchy and cannot be overthrown without the destruction of patriarchy as a whole. The relationship between patriarchy and heterosexism is important with regard to the role of gay men, for the liberation of gay men is bound up with the liberation not only of lesbians but of all women.

Just as women and men are not treated equally by patriarchy, neither are gay women and gay men. There are no neat, balancing "his and hers" oppressions; in fact, there is no such thing as men's oppression as such. Men are not put down for our maleness, although we are put down for being gays, Blacks, workers, old, young. It is true that men are limited and dehumanized by patriarchy, but we also receive the power, status, greater wealth, and feelings of superiority that patriarchy confers upon men, while women get the opposite. Feminist struggle is thus basically women's struggle, the organizing of the oppressed for their own liberation, although men have an important role to play, too.

Since women's struggle against patriarchy is different from men's, the struggles of lesbians and gay men must also be different. Both lesbians and gay men are oppressed for being gay, but gay men still receive most of the privileges of being male, while lesbians have to contend not only with gay oppression but with that of being women as well. Lesbians and gay men both suffer approximately equally, though somewhat differently, from heterosexism and can unite to fight it from similar positions. The double oppression of lesbians makes it essential that they play a leadership role in the united struggle. Lesbian feminists have an awareness of the institution of patriarchy in its anti-woman *and* its anti-gay dimension. This explains why lesbian activists are generally more radical than gay male activists. They tend to see the enemy more fully and clearly and they know that trying to win only half the battle against patriarchy—gay civil rights—will still leave them in an oppressed position as women.

Effeminate gay men experience some of the anti-woman dynamic in patriarchal culture because they exhibit behavior which is stereotypical of women in our society. But the abuse heaped on them may in addition come from the fact that they are *men* acting "like women," traitors to the Masculine Cause. Some gay men have been developing a political awareness from their situation and, proudly calling themselves sissies or faggots, make their common cause with women a primary strategic goal.

A gay man need not be abused for effeminacy in order to see the connection between gay liberation and women's liberation, however. Our analysis should make clear the need for common struggle. Men can become strong and reliable allies of women by supporting women's issues and taking responsibility for interrupting sexism in the men's world, including in male-male relationships.

Today, enough progress is being made on the civil rights front and enough tolerance is growing in some social circles so that openly gay men are being co-opted by the system. There is a tempting new bargain being offered by society in some places: you can be out of the closet if you keep your gayness in the bedroom and your consciousness low. If you are butch enough (that is, identifying with masculinity as the dominant character ideal), you can be "accepted" as openly gay and contribute toward maintaining the system despite its oppression of women, effeminate gay men, and other minorities.

I don't see a contradiction between being gay and working inside the system. Being gay and being a success in a capitalist endeavor or capitalist society have nothing to do with one another. We were never really inhibited as long as we could cover it up, which doesn't exist with other minorities. With blacks and most minorities, and women, there's no way they can disguise it...

In my own case, I've been able to work for a company that's very understanding. They don't give a crap about my personal life as long as I perform well, but I better continue to perform!...[13]

If we want to go beyond tolerance and limited acceptance to a society which liberates gayness, gay men must be solidly anti-sexist and acknowledge that lesbian feminists are taking leadership in the struggle. With a feminist perspective, we can see more clearly the problems in the gay men's world—the status hierarchy in which "butch" is put at the top and effeminacy is put at the bottom, the glorification of the large penis, the domination/submission games played in relationships. In the gay male movement we can see how masculine power-tripping can divide gay men into cliques and factions. In gay men's organizations there are not women to reconcile and heal and bridge gaps and do the million subtle bits of community-building which keep a society of mixed sexes going. This is one reason why gay men's organizations have trouble maintaining themselves well and will have trouble until they adopt feminist process and put a high value on nurturing—the nurturing of each other as men and the nurturing of the movement.[14]

A Feminist Perspective for Men

Most men—gay and heterosexual—remember tender and vulnerable moments of boyhood when we opened ourselves to another boy. While giggling together in fourth grade or swimming on long hot July afternoons, trick-or-treating on Hallowe'en night or trading baseball cards, we felt a warm buddyhood. Being close to other males, not having to keep defenses up, feeling good about other boys and about ourselves—most men can remember times like that.

Adulthood is often a different story. In our secret hearts most of us do not like ourselves as men and feel distrustful of other men as well. We show this in different ways: some of us have trouble accepting the love of other men and really believing in it; others put ourselves down as a matter of habit; some of us who are gay are cynical about the gay world and regard it as just so much pettiness and power struggle. The years since boyhood have left scars of broken dreams and dashed hopes. It's hard for us to meet a new man with the expectation that he will like us and will deal gently with us; we may keep him interested with our wit, our looks, our status, our caring—but we remain wary. He is, after all, a man.

In addition to not feeling good about ourselves as men, we have absorbed bad feelings about ourselves as gay. The homophobia which greets us everywhere—from Hollywood movies to graffiti on the walls of restrooms—nibbles away at our self-respect.

Yet another layer of bad feeling comes for many men whose consciousness has been raised about women's oppression. Not only are we carrying disappointment about the male sex (including ourselves) and hurt about our gayness, but it turns out that we are also oppressors! Guilt provides another reason to be down on ourselves. This feminist analysis is a bitter pill to swallow, because we so badly need to retain some degree of self-respect.

In such a situation it is easy to be stuck. Being stuck might mean feeling depressed, complaining about and blaming other men, adopting angry strategies for change.

Getting unstuck involves a decision and a new way of seeing. The decision is to take responsibility for oneself and one's growth as a male person. The new way of seeing is to cherish oneself as unique, special. We need to see ourselves as resourceful people who can appreciate other men's resourcefulness. We have not oppressed others because we wanted to, but because we were socialized into a system where we were expected to and it appeared necessary and because we were not encouraged to see the ways in which we exercise male privilege or fit into the scheme of institutionalized sexism or racism. Other men have hurt us not because they wanted to, but because they were scared or in some other way prevented from seeing the brother in us.

We men can help each other get unstuck. We can join together in support groups, sharing the hurts and taking the risks of vulnerability. We can remind each other in a variety of ways that we men are good, that we can be trusted, that holding each other need not be part of a sexual agenda, that we have much to be proud of. Because support groups are for supporting our growth, we can discover in them the gentle and effective ways to challenge each others' sexism. We can practice setting goals for ourselves and practice asking for help from other men in achieving them. We can practice the skills of nurturance, benefiting our lovers and the movement alike.

The life situation of gay men pushes us toward recovery of the human characteristics which are labelled "feminine." If there is no nurturing at all in a male-male relationship it will fail, and so gay men find encouragement in our daily lives to get in touch with our ability to nurture. If there is no sensitive communication between male lovers, the loving will be unsatisfying. Our need to give and receive love pushes us to get in touch with our intuition and with our feelings. This may be why sex researchers Masters and Johnson found in their study *Homosexuality in Perspective* that gay people make love more richly and with more satisfaction than heterosexual people do.[15] Without the strong heterosexist programming which prescribes what love-making should be like, gays were found by Masters and Johnson to be more flexible, more varied, more responsive to our partners, and more communicative in our love-making.

Having same-sex friends and lovers is good for growth, but it also shows up the conditioning which requires growth. In getting close to other men, gay men quickly come up against our socialized need to dominate and can find ourselves in tremendous power struggles. Clearly, gay men must deal with what power has done to us, and a committed relationship with another man is an excellent place to work through this conditioning, especially if there is help from a support group. Gay men sometimes enter a time of celibacy as an alternative to acting on our need to dominate or be dominated, while we are in the process of countering our socialization. In any case, men's conditioning to dominate must be worked through so gay men can free ourselves and relate to women unoppressively.

Effeminacy, or, Why are heterosexual men's wrists so stiff?

Many men remember, as boys, being called "girls" or "sissies" because they were unusually thin, or fat, or not competitive in sports, or had a high-pitched voice; others had little facial or body hair, or had pretty curls, or were graceful with their bodies. Some men have as adults affected dress or styles usually associated with women in this society: the first male on the block to carry a purse or wear an earring is bound to get some comments or looks which range from quizzical to hostile.

Effeminacy—men acting like or having traits ascribed to women—is a major controversy in gay circles. The gay sub-culture resembles the mainstream society in putting down effeminacy whether it is expressed subtly or in the extreme of drag or transvestites. Drag queens and others who are "swishy" have for a long time been at the bottom of the gay world's status ladder, and the celebration of the butch style seems recently to be increasing.[16] Some lesbian feminists challenge the caricature of womanhood which is represented in the performance of many drag queens.

On the other hand, there are gay men who argue that it is patriarchy which makes men afraid to be sissies and that gay pride includes the defiant embracing of what used to be a negative image; just as gay men can call each other faggots with a sense of warm brotherhood, so a sissy movement can grow which delights in not having to strike the masculine pose. Like the "Black is beautiful" slogan in the Black Civil Rights Movement of the '60s which contradicted internalized racism by affirming what had been scorned, so there can now be "fairy gatherings" in which gay men seek a new blend of feminism, new age politics, spirituality, and gayness.[17]

I'll never forget the first time I wore a dress at a party. At first I was nervous, but then I relaxed and started to feel so *free*. I danced more gracefully than I ever have, was funnier in conversation, and in general felt so light and good. I later realized that getting out of men's clothes gave me permission to be free of the masculine posture, and to be more myself. Even though it was a mixed party of gays and non-gays, I felt freer that night than I do in a gay bar!

In this story we can see a man reaching for androgyny—for his whole self not confined by sex roles—by wearing a dress. Since wearing men's clothes is all wrapped up with the rigidities of traditional masculinity, wearing women's clothes can mean breaking free. Nudity might do the same for some; for this man, the long dress symbolized lightness and grace and therefore helped his own party spirit to fly.

There is a political dimension to this as well. The cool and tough posture of masculinity is part of the picture of the oppression of women. When men realize how that oppression hurts us all and identify with the struggle of women, we can show that identification symbolically by effeminate style and dress. Since so much of anti-gay male feeling seems linked to woman-hating, it is especially appropriate for gay men to show common cause with women through letting our feminine side out of the closet.

Whether or not we are gay, gay men can be more fully ourselves when we give up the masculine straitjacket. Dancing and other forms of limp-wristedness like crying in public and giggling and skipping down the street can all mean getting in touch with an expanded sense of self, can all show the inner security which refuses to bow to convention.

There is another side of effeminacy, however, which does not reflect a free spirit. Weinberg and Williams, in their study of *Male Homosexuals*, asked over 2400 gay men whether they look and act effeminate, and then compared the responses to how the men described their psychological well-being. The men who rated themselves high in effeminacy were lowest in self-acceptance and in stability of self-concept, and they were highest in psychosomatic symptoms and depression.[18] Because of the way the world often looks at effeminacy, many men find that it is not a fully satisfactory way of presenting themselves—an understandable response when one sees the scorn for effeminacy not only in heterosexual society but in the gay community as well.

To further complicate the issue, it is our impression that class background has to do with effeminacy. The motorcycle riders who frequent leather bars and pose as tough guys seem disproportionately to be middle to upper-middle class in background. There is a tradition in the English gay world, which gay novelist E.M. Forster and others describe, of middle/upper-class men deliberately seeking lovers among the presumably rougher and more virile working-class men. If, because of being brought up in the cultivated upper classes, one feels oneself to be preoccupied with "feminine pursuits," one can at least seek sexual partners who will put one back in touch with the masculine side of oneself. But these well-off men who, on both sides of the Atlantic, have a hankering for "rough trade," may well have little or no effeminacy in their personal manner—they already feel too removed, perhaps, from their male identity by the social situation they have been born into. Their focus, their direction, is masculinity.

Drag queens, on the other hand, seem largely to be working-class in background. Many working-class boys see adults in polarized sex roles, and they often see working-class men, abused by the class system, take out their frustrations on their wives and children. Seeing a harsh version of aggressive masculinity, a boy may identify with femininity in reaction to the aggressiveness. Ted, a working-class drag queen interviewed in the documentary film *Word Is Out*, reflected on his own choice:

> *Femininity to me seems to say passivity and a real idea of where a man wants a woman to be—like a male identification of what a woman is. A lot of early drag feelings I had, and I think a lot of boys have, were around those passive female roles....* [19]

We are guessing that, because masculinity and femininity are more polarized in parts of the working class than in most of the middle/upper class, gay working-class boys are more often made to feel that they must choose, and, given the choice, identify with women rather than men. Effeminacy becomes, then, not an expanded self which is already firmly anchored in acceptance of one's maleness, but an *alternative self* which is all too vulnerable to the slings and arrows of a sexist society (and a sexist gay men's culture). As such, it easily becomes rigid in a way that offends some feminist women, who insist that such a caricature buys into patriarchy instead of refusing to cooperate with it.

Where does this leave a gay man who is trying to decide whether to pierce his ears or change his style in another effeminate way? As we have pointed out, effeminacy can be a political statement, and some men may want to put on a show to zap the thinking of heterosexuals looking on, or to raise the consciousness of closeted gays. As a political statement, effeminacy can express solidarity with women. But this can be a situational use of effeminacy. What about a personal change in style?

The main guideline we suggest is whether the behavior is simply a reaction against masculinity or, more positively, a step toward androgyny— a human style which goes beyond sex-role stereotypes. Reacting against masculinity is natural because so many of us know we have been hurt by it, but flipping to the other side of the sex-role division laid out by patriarchy is not a solution, even though it may be an intermediate stage. A reasonable goal for a feminist gay man is to transcend the feminine/masculine categories. That involves accepting who one simply is—male—and not wasting energy on rejecting or feeling guilty about it. It is similar to the growth stage reached by anti-racist whites when they finally realize that it is okay to be white. Being white is not the problem; what racism has done with whiteness is the problem. Effeminacy, in short, is limiting and rigid when it is rooted in self-hatred and a rejection of who one is in fact—a man. Effeminacy liberates when it is reaching toward androgyny from a base of self-acceptance, including acceptance of oneself as a man.

G. Talbott is a working-class Black man who for years was a drag queen, then decided to begin saving for surgery so he could become a transsexual. His cross-dressing became elaborate and he could often pass for a woman. He insisted on being called "Gwendolyn."

After losing touch with him for a year, I ran into him at a movement event; he was informally dressed in a way that was neither particularly feminine nor masculine. I tried to catch up on the news. "I'm not Gwendolyn any more," he said, "just G. And I'm not saving for surgery any more."

"Why?" I asked.

"I found out about androgyny, dear," G. said, "and I know the world isn't ready, but I'm willing to be the first."

Relating to heterosexual and bisexual men

Letting the gayness flow and developing a lifestyle consistent with our best understanding of liberation is both a delight and a big job. It involves a lot of time hanging out with other gays, playing, struggling, doing political work, giving and getting support. Many gay men will find that, at least for a portion of our lives, all our closest associates and most involving activities will be gay. Gay men may need a separatist period, as lesbian feminist women do, in order to make sure we put first things first in our lives.

As gay men grow in self-confidence and gay pride, however, it is appropriate to give leadership to broader social change efforts. Gay men can be a powerful and leading force in the men's movement as a whole, because of our commitment to other men. Our oppression as gays can give special insight into the nature of patriarchy. By challenging heterosexual men to deal with their homophobia and to release suppressed gay feelings they may have, gay men present a powerful challenge to patriarchy, which needs men to continue to be masculine and especially to control women. Gay men's experience also helps us to make connections between patriarchy and other forms of oppression. Gays can organize campaigns against the military, for example, highlighting the connections between masculinity, violence, and authority.

Because anti-sexist gay men see ourselves as fierce allies of women, we can take responsibility for interrupting men's sexism whether or not women are present. Gays can take responsibility for finding support for heterosexual men when the women they were relating to leave them to become lesbians or separatists. Men in this situation need the support of brothers to help them deal with their feelings, to keep feeling good about themselves, and to understand why separatism is important for women. Gay men should be prepared to take the initiative in these situations, to step in and offer support or help the heterosexual men find support. This is enormously important to women as well as to the men concerned because it is easier for a woman to end a primary relationship with a man she cares about if she knows his brothers will be there to support him. Moreover, it can be a very important experience for a man to realize that he can get effective loving support from another man.

When my woman lover shared with me that she wanted to sleep with another woman, it was a terrifying thing for me. (We had done much talking about eventually becoming lovers with others of the same gender, but this was *real*—right here and now.) Fortunately we were in a situation where each of us had plenty of support. Without my asking, as soon as my men's support group realized I was in need, they immediately surrounded me, carried me away to a quiet space and listened to me share my fears, insecurity, anger, and hurt. Having the support of that group of men made all the difference to me. I was able to sort out what was reminding me of ways I had been hurt in the past, and to think clearly about the present situation. After a couple of hours, I was able to return to my lover and actively encourage her to continue the exploration of her sexuality and her humanness.

A warning: gay men need to be thoughtful about the men we are considering giving support to, and thoughtful about ourselves. If the gay man feels drawn to spend much of his time with heterosexual men and often falls in love with them, he may still be carrying the feeling that gay men are not really all right. There may be some feeling of inferiority which sets him up to be exploited by a heterosexual man who is glad to use a gay man for support during crises but then leaves as soon as the next heterosexual woman appears in his life. One way out of this problem is for gay men to take the initiative in setting up structures to help heterosexual men support each other, such as the "uncoupling co-ops" which were organized by the Men's Resource Center of Seattle, in which men who lost their wives/lovers helped each other not to rush into another sexist relationship, but to take time to face up to their masculine condition.

Most men who identify as heterosexual probably have some gay sexual feelings, and of course men who identify as bisexual are acknowledging that they can relate sexually to men as well as women. This brings both hope and reservations for gay men. It is encouraging because one meaning of gay liberation is to liberate *gayness*, wherever it is being stifled; it is wonderful to be a part of that. It is also frightening because there have been so many cases of rejection. Rejection frequently occurs when a non-gay man explores his sexuality with a gay man and becomes frightened when he realizes on a gut level that oppression really exists and that this oppression may affect him if he continues his exploration of gayness. In fear he backs away. The gay man may care deeply for the non-gay and be hurt and confused by the departures.

A group of bisexual men in Movement for a New Society struggled with this problem at a national gathering and created a set of guidelines for men who are exploring their gayness:

1) Take responsibility for your own gayness; do not give it to your gay lover to "take care of" and let him do the thinking and listening and suffering through your fears. It's your sexuality. Take charge of it and take initiative in getting support from other people for your development and growth.

2) Realize that when the fears come up you may feel like taking shelter in a relationship with a woman. Realize that the oppression will push you in that direction and arm yourself against it by deciding to put priority attention on your friendships with men, emotional as well as physical. Some bisexuals have found it useful to abstain from new sexual relationships with women until they feel secure in their gayness.

Ben and I had been good friends for several years and decided together to work in the men's movement. He consciously worked on his homophobia and was very supportive of my gayness. He then decided to explore his own gayness and, one night when we were sleeping together, made love with me. He seemed so relaxed and delighted, and felt like celebrating afterwards.

Four days later he fell madly in love with a woman and spent all his free time with her for a couple of months. It was years before he could admit that he'd experienced a fear reaction to his gay lovemaking.

---

3) Don't let your gay lover defer to a heterosexual relationship you may already be in. If he's holding back it may because society says that a man-woman relationship is more important than a man-man relationship.

These guidelines for bisexuals are reasonable for gay men to push for in a relationship with a non-gay. Loving a non-gay can be very confusing: it seems wise to be wary, yet growthful to be vulnerable; a gay man deserves to be loved without reservation and fear, yet at this point in history homophobia seems everywhere (in gay men as well). Help is available in deciding what to do:

My bisexual lover and I were having troubles in our relationship and wondering if we should drop the sexual part. We were confused, and both of us could see arguments pro and con. So we convened a group of people who knew us well and put the issue to them. As they questioned us and shared their thinking we became a lot more clear, and were able to make a decision about next steps in our relationship.[20]

Married gays

Because of the strong heterosexual assumptions that most of us grew up with, many gay people have been, or still are, married. We have already mentioned women who cannot openly proclaim their lesbian identities because of economic dependency or children. There are gay men as well who lead double lives. This is often easier for men because of the greater freedom that we exercise in this society, but no less damaging psychologically.

Some gay people, both male and female, have chosen to stay married while at the same time working actively and openly in the struggle for gay liberation. These people may have known of their gayness before marriage and discussed it with their spouses-to-be, or they may have discovered it later on and had to go through the coming-out process while involved in another, heterosexual, primary relationship. The marriage partner may be heterosexually identified, or also gay, or moving in that direction. Whatever the case, there may be reasons for staying married that can contribute to the positive growth of both parties.[21]

If children are involved, both adults may be committed to co-parenting those children. It is clear to us that parenting has little or nothing to do with the parents' expression of their sexuality and that often two people who married with the expectation of having and raising children should do so, regardless of their sexual preference.

In our vision of a future society, we mentioned communal households where people of all sexual preferences will have a hand in raising young people. Gay people who are presently married and who live in such households can become the models for such future visions.

This does not mean that we support the concept of heterosexual, monogamous marriage as our society currently defines and accepts it. The married gay people we speak of here are struggling to find alternatives to the nuclear family model, and a communal household where several adults share the economic and child-rearing functions seems to be one positive alternative that is available to us right now.

There is no rational reason to give up a warm, loving, and supportive relationship with another human being simply because society has chosen to define it in a certain way by labeling it "marriage." Some gay people have done a lot of work with their spouses and their same-sex lovers to come to a balance that they find good for them. Though such relationships are rare in this society, they do exist. To say that they are permanent seems unrealistic, but to say they are impossible seems equally so.

Many married gay people prefer staying in the closet rather than continually defending their lifestyle and relationships to other gays. To have to do this is counter-productive and takes energy away from other parts of the struggle.

A gay man or lesbian who is out and doing political work, thinking, struggling, and changing, open to questioning, self-challenge and evaluation, and who is also married, deserves support and not criticism. One of the things the gay culture offers is variety and the freedom to choose. We do not need to demand that all gay people have similar lifestyles in order to be politically involved in the struggle for liberation.

Faggot fathers

It's amusing but sad to hear homophobes say that gayness must not be encouraged because the human race needs reproduction to ensure its future. There are millions of lesbians and gay men in the United States who are the parents of children and who are raising them conscientiously. Little is written about them because gay parents are especially vulnerable if they are open.

The same public interest law group that recently won a lesbian mother custody of her child also recently lost an attempt for me to have any legal access, much less than custody, to my daughter. In fact, we were completely powerless. My daughter's mother fled Oregon, in the face of a restraining order, and obtained a custody order in another state. I now have no legal recourse, and negotiations will take years, if they can happen at all.[22]

This gay father has suffered an important loss. Many gay men have experienced the rich satisfaction and delight of loving children and being loved by them. Youngsters often have the ability to bring out the playfulness in grownups, to brush aside the stuffiness and self-importance we adults collect and provoke directness and spontaneity. Their fresh perspective on the world is a source of insight for everyone. Some gay men who desire this but do not want to father children move into collective households where children are present and take an active role in care and play.

Parenting is not all happiness, of course. One special problem for faggot fathers comes when a child brings home the homophobia of the general culture.

"I think all gays should be burned and killed," my ten-year-old son would say, then look at me intently to gauge my reaction. Or, while dressing in the morning: "I don't want to wear *that*. People would think I'm gay!"

I responded in as relaxed and lighthearted a way as I could, not being certain what this testing meant and not wanting to escalate things into a heavy number. In a couple months he gave it up and now cuddles and loves me as well as ever.

Since rearing children in a homophobic world is not easy, gay men who are caring for youngsters need support. They need to think about how they will handle it if friends of the children learn about the gayness, or if their child denies it or in other ways shows embarrassment and confusion about the adult's orientation. Some gay fathers are finding each other through married gay men's support groups. In Philadelphia, through advertisements in newspapers and gay periodicals, gay married men are getting together and starting groups that can become primary support places.

With such support, a solid, open relationship, and a little luck, the children of gay fathers can be comfortable with their friends and become wonderful allies for us.

I asked my six-year-old daughter one day how she handled it when people in her first grade said anti-gay things, like calling someone "faggot." She said she told them to stop it, and if that didn't work, she went to her teacher and the teacher stood beside her while she again insisted that it stop.

"The others sometimes say, 'It's all right, Linda, because everyone knows that gay people aren't nice.' And then *I* say, 'They are so nice. My daddy's gay, and *he's* nice.'"

A gay male friend of mine came out to his nine-year-old son with a great deal of anxiety. After a long explanation that included more than a few tears on the father's part, the son said, "Well, I guess this means I ought to be nicer to Mark, since he's your lover." After more discussion, the boy said, "Daddy, I don't care if you make it with a light socket as long as you love me!"

A liberated movement for liberation

The gay men's culture is a fascinating world, changing and growing as it interacts with mainstream society. We find vitality and support there. Where "respectable" people (and Puritans of the left and right) find decadence, we find some meaning and life. When they call us to leave the cracks of society where our gayness has been expressed and to clean up our act, we reply: We are in the cracks of society because you put us there and, having made something good for ourselves in that space, we will leave it only when you make the mainstream a liberated space for all peoples. We will solve the problems in the gay men's culture and build alternatives to the practices which hurt us as we grow in pride and as society changes as a whole. Let love flow more abundantly!

Gay Spirit

When we were born they tried to cover our eyes
They tried to tell us all what to see
We are discovering this did not work
For we are born to be free.

Chorus:
There's a gay spirit singing in our hearts
Leading us through these troubled times
A gay spirit moving 'round this land
Calling us to a time of open love.

When we were born they tried to put us in a cage
Then tell our bodies what to feel
We have chosen to feel all the truth
That our bodies do reveal.

We are no strangers to all the pain
That comes with fighting for our love
We are the outlaws in this lovesick land
Whose crime has only been to care.

You run and tell that ol' patriarch
We're no longer blind to his ways
You run and tell him we are stealin' all the keys
To all those prisons he has made.
Sometimes it gets too hard to feel all the joy
In the face of all the pain we see
But there is a healing place within our hearts
It's coming alive in you and me.

—Charlie Murphy[23]

Chapter VII

We Can Make the Changes

This book has presented a detailed analysis of how and why heterosexism operates, a vision of a society free of sexual oppression, and strategic thinking on how lesbians and gay men can develop a movement for liberation which can unite allies to bring about fundamental changes.

Some of the strategic thinking has probably struck some readers as too grand, too ambitious. We admit to a certain uppity-ness. We propose, as one might expect of gays, an outrageous revolution. We think our optimism is more than pretension; the social changes we are proposing are for a movement in which the political is personal, the personal, political. Other movements did not encourage personal change and use the energy thus freed; the outward, institutional changes were the only ones on their agenda. We believe in combining the two dimensions. It is not easy. A few years of practice, with little theory, have not provided a magic carpet. But we have experienced times of synergy—when the whole became greater than the sum of the parts—because so much of our selves was available to the common project, and so much of the fruits of the project was available to our selves.

In this chapter, we focus attention on unlocking the energy which is within non-gay allies and within lesbians and gay men, energy which is now suppressed by homophobia, by classism, by racism, and by the other burdens society lays on us. First we offer suggestions for moving toward a new, more human sexuality for us all. Then we discuss next steps for non-gays, people of goodwill who wish to become strong and intelligent allies and, in the process, to become more fully human themselves. And last, we propose in detail a number of next steps for lesbians and gay men.

Liberating sexuality

In sex, perhaps more than in any other area of human activity, it is vital that we avoid moralism. Our Puritan-soaked culture has made a special point of righteousness regarding sexuality, and radicals sometimes retain that attitude in stating the "correct" policy on sex. On the other hand, today's "free sexuality" has become a creed that puts particular pressure on women. Whether a specific sexual practice is right for the individual depends on that person's background, present needs, and sense of priorities. These factors are not easy to sort out, and all the judgmentalism in the world will not help. In exploring how you wish to express your sexuality, you might consider the following suggestions:

Look at your sexual sharing in the context of personal growth toward autonomy and self-actualization. If you are moving from heterosexual to homosexual loving, be aware that you may continue to model dependent behavior you have learned; try to get support to move toward freedom through working on your feelings and developing a new non-dependent model.

Let same-sex relationships be emotionally as deep and full as those you may have enjoyed with the opposite sex. It is patriarchy, not us, which defines gays and gayness simply in terms of sex!

Learn from the eroticism of children; notice how babies experience their sexuality from head to foot. That potential is still there for us as adults.

Answer children's questions about sexuality in a relaxed, open manner. Do not hide your sexuality from them.

The beach was fairly crowded that day and a lot of people seemed to enjoy the picture of the six-year-old boy and the grown man romping together in the water, having a delightful time.

We got tired and cold and decided to rest on a blanket. Michael had goose bumps and was shivering. The sun went behind the clouds, so I invited him to lie on my stretched-out body to warm up faster. We put a towel on top, and he hugged my body close. I became erect, which he noticed and asked about. I reminded him that his penis sometimes grew and got stiff, and that was what was happening to me.

Michael's eyes grew big as saucers. "You mean grown men have that happen to them too?"

I began to wonder how much anxiety children carry around because they lack the easy opportunity to learn about bodies and what things mean.

Explore body experiences. Massage is a way to get in touch with pleasure and to liberate sensual/sexual energies. Massage is sensual communication between two people which expresses direct caring; it is often a centering experience as well as a social one.

Explore your sexual feelings by masturbating. Masturbation can be the safest and freest way of discovering and developing our sexual feelings. Since male domination of women most certainly includes attempted control of female sexuality, ranging from the myth of the vaginal orgasm to clitoridectomy (removal of the clitoris),[1] masturbation is important for women as a method of creating and defining our own sexuality in a situation we control. Masturbation is for pleasing ourselves and loving ourselves. Women often are taught that our bodies, especially our genitals, are disgusting, dirty, and ugly. Masturbation is a way of rejecting this lesson and becoming familiar with, enjoying, and loving our bodies and our sexuality.[2] In addition, masturbation is an excellent way to appreciate and become more familiar with a same-sex body (which is helpful in the transition from heterosexuality to gayness). Knowing how to please ourselves sexually gives us a starting point in exploring sex with another person. Also, being able to satisfy our own sexual needs gives us sexual independence and takes away the pressure to get involved in relationships in order to satisfy sexual needs.

Watch out: do you use sex as a cover for other needs, such as affection, attention, touching, and reassurance? If you think you use sex in this way, try celibacy for a period of time while actively meeting those needs in other ways. This will help you find out what your authentic sexual needs are, in contrast to your cultural programming.

If you have difficulty initiating or entering into sexual relationships, tell yourself—and your journal, mirror, friend, or therapist—"I am an attractive, desirable, sexual person." Experience yourself as a sexual person (masturbate, dance sexually, etc.), although it may be scary or embarrassing. Tell others when you are attracted to them and notice when others may be attracted to you. If you are a woman looking for another woman, don't "wait for the man to make the first move."

In relationships, be experimental about sex. Try not engaging in genital sex for awhile; concentrate on other aspects of the relationship, on other ways to express love and on expanding your sensual contact. Make an agreement with your partner that lovemaking does not need to push inexorably toward a foregone conclusion but can pause or be given up in order to respond to other needs.

I'll never forget the time when my lover paused in the middle of sex and asked what I was feeling. He gave me a look of such safety and acceptance that I let my feelings come to the surface—feelings of resentment and anger that I hadn't expressed earlier. I started to tell him, and he encouraged me to continue. Next thing I knew I was pounding the pillow and attacking him verbally, while he just lay there quietly paying attention to me. Sometimes I was half-embarrassed by what I was saying, because it wasn't really balanced truth; just a rush of feelings. But he reassured me and so I kept on pounding and attacking until I dissolved into tears. He then held me in his arms, while I cried and cried with my head against his chest. After a while the tears subsided and I drifted into the sweetest sleep imaginable.

That was such powerful loving he gave me that night; it drew us much closer to each other.

Try to eroticize everyday life, to break down the watertight compartments between "romance" and "real life." Touching people out of affection is reassuring because it extends to everybody; it is very different from sexual game-playing.

Realize that all these steps and others need to be taken with great humility, because of the little that we know about sexuality. Furthermore, since women are often conditioned to repress their sexuality and men to be compulsively sexual, different steps may be appropriate for each. Patriarchy has taken over sexuality and shaped it; as we move away from that tradition and take charge of our sexuality in the context of building a new society, we are bound to make mistakes. We would do well to regard our sexual life as a series of experiments from which we can learn and slowly develop a theory of what human sexuality can really be like.

NEXT STEPS FOR
NON-GAY WOMEN AND MEN

Allies

Gay people need solid allies. We do not want guilty hangers-on; guilt is not a reliable motivation for giving support, nor is it a motive which comes from the center of the self.

An ally is one who keeps informed of political positions put forward by the lesbian and gay communities, and who seeks dialogue with the goal of incorporating into her or his own social change work those positions which make sense. An ally includes lesbian and gay men's organizations in conferences, coalitions, and roundtables and is a visible presence at gatherings and demonstrations called by gays. An ally reaches out to people to whom lesbian and gay organizations have little access, in order to raise their consciousness and make specific proposals for changes.

A young friend of mine came up to me after Friends meeting recently and asked if I would read something he had written. When I said, "Sure," he explained that he had been elected the leader of his Boy Scout patrol and had written up some rules for the behavior of the group. I wondered why he had chosen me—until I got to rule number five, which read something like this: "No one in this patrol is to call anyone else a faggot or queer because these words are insulting to gay men, and gay men are some of the best people in our society." He looked at me anxiously and asked, "Do you think that's firm enough?" Whew! I was blown away. And to think that all that time I had been worried about his response to my lesbianism! I told him the statement was great and asked why he had decided to write it. "Well," he explained, "I know that you're gay, and George and Bill are gay, and Rick is gay, and you're all really neat people, and I just didn't think it was fair."

An ally who is committed, on his or her own behalf as well as ours, brings consciousness of liberation into everyday life. Here are some specific ways allies we know have gone about this:

1. Assume that, wherever you go, there are closeted gay people who are wondering how safe the environment is for them. Provide safety by making it clear that you accept gayness.

2. Realize that the cultural oppression of gays is perpetuated in social situations where the only hugging and physical affection is heterosexual. You can refrain from heterosexual touching and/or be affectionate with someone of the same sex.

3. Challenge heterosexism whether or not gays are present; do not always leave it to gays to do it. Sometimes it is the assumptions as well as anti-gay statements which need challenging—such as: divided sleeping arrangements between females and males rules out the possibility of sexual interaction. This assumption supports the invisibility of gays.

4. When speaking of your (heterosexual) lover, point out that s/he is of the opposite sex, implying that s/he need not be. Or, in those situations where it is unclear whether you are loving a woman or a man, leave it that way.

5. Do not assume that you know it all. *Listen* to gays. Read gay analysis and learn about the reality of gay oppression.

6. Challenge your own homophobia:
     be physically affectionate with others of the same sex
     enjoy gay culture: music, plays, films, poetry, fiction, and publications
     try wearing gay liberation buttons and the button which reads, "How dare you assume I'm heterosexual?"

7. If people jump to the conclusion that you are gay because of your friendship with gay people, because you are reading a gay magazine or because you are being affectionate with a friend of the same sex, resist the impulse to point out that you are not gay. Be willing to experience the oppression that gays suffer rather than take advantage of heterosexual privilege.

8. Get close to a gay person if appropriate. Some gays will be wary of putting a lot of energy into a relationship with you because we have been ripped off by non-gays in the past. Realize that gays often put more energy into friendships with people of the same sex than non-gays do, so be prepared for that and allow the relationship to mean a lot to you, too.

9. Get in touch with the gayness that may be within you. Realize that heterosexuality was not a free choice for you but was imposed on you by this society. Honor your whole being by feeling your own gayness. It is unwise to have sex with someone for purely political

reasons, because you think you *ought* to be gay or bisexual. When politics is the only reasons for sex, you can easily exploit the other person and abuse yourself. If you believe, as the writers do, that it is patriarchal homophobic conditioning that is suppressing your gayness, it makes sense to remove that block so that you will *want* gay love and not think you should force yourself to experience it. Here are ways in which some people have successfully worked on removing the blocks to gay loving:

—Spend time in predominantly gay groups.

—Become emotionally close to people of the same sex.

—Sleep and and be sensual with friends of the same sex; share massages.

—Remember times when you have been scared by the idea of homosexuality; recall and release those feelings, thereby diminishing their hold on you.

—Remember all the times you have heard negative things about homosexuality, and assert out loud what is really true.

—Remember times when you were hurt by people of the same sex that led you to distrust them, and release your feelings of anger.

—Fantasize making love with a friend of the same sex.

—Talk with your friends about gayness; confide about your fears, even the embarrassing details.

—Once you are in touch with your gay feelings, consider setting a goal of making love with someone of the same sex within a certain period of time. It can be a frightening thing to do for the first time, so if you do not push, it probably will not happen. Do not be rigid about the time limit, but use it to push yourself to make opportunities.

Heterosexual women claim their own space

We believe that one of the things that will be most helpful in the struggle to change society is a raised consciousness on the part of heterosexual women about the role they now occupy and how it needs to change if patriarchy is to be outwitted in the end. But we maintain that it is virtually impossible for any woman to recognize all the ways that (hetero)sex is oppressive until she has stepped out of it for a while and taken a look at it from the outside. Thus we recommend that each woman have a space in her life in which she puts her primary energy into women.

The large majority of non-lesbian women have one-to-one, intimate daily connections with their oppressors (men) on which their immediate happiness, security, and survival depend. (This relationship to oppressors is also true for a smaller percentage of many other groups: working class, Third World, religious, and ethnic.) As a result, most women and the men they relate to fall very deeply into behavior patterns that reinforce sex oppression. They reinforce each other in these patterns because of their dependence on each other (and on that way of relating) for survival.

Since dependency and oppression are so tangled together, it is especially hard for heterosexual women to be aware of their situation while they are living in the middle of it. Serving a man has been part of their experience all their lives and is the "normal" way of life for almost every woman they know; they accept it as the way things naturally are and don't realize that it is oppressive or that things could be different.

Moving in the direction of having a separate space is a big change for most women, and it can come gradually. Going against basic assumptions in the home, like who does housework or child care, may be a first step that leads a woman to spending regular time in a women's group. Allowing her to feel angry about those assumptions may motivate her to get support for change from other women. Many heterosexual women already have women's space in their lives that is valuable to them, but they don't necessarily think of it as women's space: talking over coffee with neighbors, mutual support with co-workers, spending time at a bridge club or with a close friend. Acknowledging how important these times with women are and insisting on them in her life is a very big step for a woman to take. Thus, separatism as we are talking about it does not have to begin with a radical plunge into a whole different world.

Separatism doesn't necessarily mean being sexual with other women, either, although to do so is natural and positive—a growing part of loving women and being women-identified.

We are not recommending that a woman never rely on a man for anything, but that women have a period of not needing men at all in order to break out of the strong socialization to need them *all* the time. In the same way, the socialization to put men first is so deep and powerful that until a woman has said *No* completely for a while, she is not truly free to choose whether to say *Yes* or *No*.

I was trying to break my compulsive habit of always responding positively to any request made of me by my male lover. I told myself innumerable times that I was free to refuse if I wished. In my head I truly knew that I had that choice. Yet every time, on the spot, I always said, "Yes," and it would not even occur to me to think that I might refuse until afterwards.

Every woman can find a time in her life when she truly is separate from men, and this will help her to be a much more valuable ally for gays as well as a more centered human being herself. It's not possible for every woman to do it immediately, but women in all walks of life *have* made that choice. It has been a scary, exhilarating, hopeful, powerful process—and worth it.

NEXT STEPS FOR
LESBIANS AND GAY MEN

Unlearning the lies

Even though many of us have come out and made connections with other gays and feel good about our gayness, we still suffer from internalized oppression. For example, our attitudes towards gay people of the opposite sex often reflect the lies we have heard all our lives, but managed to unlearn about our own sex. The effects of internalized oppression are numerous. Feeling that we cannot trust anyone is often the result of years of being told that we are dangerous and untrustworthy; feeling lonely, that we do not belong anywhere, is the result of years of being told that we are different; feeling scared even in safe situations is the result of years of hiding and protecting ourselves. These are examples of internalized oppression that we need to help each other clean out.

One way to discover the lies about gays and homosexuality that are active in our culture is simple, and can be done alone, with a friend, or in a consciousness-raising group: list what you like about being a lesbian or gay man, and then what you hate about being gay or about other gays. Enjoy the first list, and consider the second list carefully. As you do so you will probably realize that all the items on the second list are ways we have been forced to respond to being oppressed, or they are the scars of past oppression. They are not genuine characteristics of being lesbian or gay.

Being with other lesbians or gay men is invaluable. If you have been isolated from gays or are just coming out, make a special effort to find places to be with other gays. In addition to the gay bars, almost every larger city has a gay community center, counseling center, coffeehouse, switchboard, or hot-line that can provide information on gay educational, political, and social activities. Many cities have lesbian services in addition to mixed gay ones. Lesbian groups and activities can usually be found through women's centers.

If you can't make contact in your home community, try to attend gay conferences. For example, state-wide gay pride conferences are held in Pennsylvania. Quaker lesbians now have regional and national meetings. Lesbians in Colorado had their first state-wide gathering in the autumn of 1979. The number of conferences grows each year.

If you meet others who are gay and you do not have a gay group in your area, start one. You might begin your support group by telling coming-out stories; they have a remarkably liberating effect.[3]

If you have the opportunity, live collectively with other gay men or lesbians; such a living experience can feel very freeing.

Read lesbian and gay literature. We need to envelop ourselves in positive lesbian and gay images. If your area doesn't have a gay, feminist, or progressive bookstore, you can order books and records from Giovanni's Room bookstore, 345 S. 12th St., Philadelphia, PA 19107.

I remember my first lesbian concert: I was so excited. I heard love songs sung by a woman to women. I heard a song about coming out to your mother. And I sat in a room with hundreds of lesbians— more than I had ever seen before.

Lesbian concerts are now common in large cities, but gay men's concerts are still infrequent and small. Olivia Records has produced many women's records. Some gay men's records are appearing; a popular one is Charlie Murphy's "Catch the Fire."[4]

Unlearning the lies and acting on a whole, healthy image of ourselves not only means we can live happier lives, but it also allows us to unify as a political force. It is a key part of a feminist, gay revolution.

Increasing our political awareness

As we have shown, gay oppression is not an isolated phenomenon; therefore we believe that to achieve gay liberation we must change society completely. As we organize for gay civil rights we must *educate people about heterosexism*. Those who believe it is enough to pass a few laws and counter a few stereotypes must be shown that, on the contrary, our oppression is a basic and necessary part of capitalism and patriarchy.

Gay civil rights groups or radical caucuses within such groups can educate themselves and their less radical members through literature, workshops, and study groups. An organization with a steady influx of new members would do well to set up monthly or quarterly introductory workshops. At such meetings each person can share why s/he is interested, what s/he thinks of the organization, what particular political work s/he may want to pursue, and the development of her/his analysis of gay oppression. A brief history of the organization and a statement of its strategy can be given. A good way to illustrate the significance of gay oppression is to ask participants to name the causes and effects of anti-gay attitudes and display interconnections on a "web" chart. Or the participants can take a few minutes to think about what a society free from gay oppression would look like and then share their thoughts.

A study group can serve to keep an organization's thinking developing, to explore issues in more depth than is possible at a business meeting, to share knowledge, to relate personal experiences to political issues, and to open up communication between members with different experiences.[5]

A series of short, non-rhetorical articles is an excellent tool for introducing gays and non-gays alike to the need for gay liberation. The creation of one- or two-page articles on such topics as "Who Benefits from Gay Oppression?" "Gay Liberation and Sex Roles," "How Society Hurts Gays," "How Gay Oppression Hurts Everyone," and "Visions of a Society Free of Gay Oppression" would make a most useful contribution to the gay movement. They could be distributed separately, or together as a "Gay Liberation Packet."

Articles such as these could help us spread a gay-feminist perspective in our work outside the gay community. An emphasis on visions or on how oppression hurts us all will often make our radical ideas exciting to "conservative" people. We will not create a new society or end gay oppression by convincing ordinary citizens that we are harmless. Rather we must show them that society harms them in the same ways that it harms us.

Building alternative institutions

Even with political education, gay rights organizing is not enough. We need to build new institutions and make direct attacks on patriarchy.

Alternative institutions should serve the needs of a diverse gay community yet maintain a radical political orientation. Educational programs like those described above also develop the radical character of gay institutions. Counter-institutions such as lesbian and gay men's community centers, coffeehouses, hot-lines, bookstores, and legal services create community identity and demonstrate how unmet needs can be filled.

Some events these institutions could organize are:

—creativity evenings, in which members of the community share their dancing, poetry, music, theater
—programs of all types by traveling and local lesbian and gay male cultural workers/performers
—workshops on issues of concern in the community, e.g., police harassment, sexuality, children
—skills workshops in self-defense, street theater, democratic decision making, car repair....

Counter-institutions should always be aware of how and *why* the needs they meet are created and then ignored by this society. For example, legal services for lesbian mothers facing custody problems would not be needed in a free society.

Finally, new institutions should be structured to empower all the individuals involved. Decisions should be made collectively by those immediately affected, not by a hierarchy. Each individual should be given support to contribute her/his utmost and to learn and practice new skills.

Lesbians and gay men each need to develop our autonomous programs. These could be connected to women's and men's liberation centers, respectively; or, if the gay men are sufficiently anti-sexist to respect the lesbians' need for self-determination, creating a joint gay community center would be an excellent use of resources and would promote greater political unity. Lesbians and gay men could have separate office and social meeting space but alternate in the use of large or expensive facilities. Male gay groups should not add a few women and then call themselves "the gay center" nor think that they are serving the lesbian community as well as their own. Both groups can have some activities open to not-yet-gay people, while continuing to meet the needs for an all-gay environment most of the time.

Campaigning for specific changes

Direct-action campaigns which attack a particular injustice through a series of public protests are very important to the gay liberation movement. Of all kinds of organizing these campaigns generally have the greatest freedom to be militant and will most strongly resist co-optation. A small group (four to eight people) is all that's needed to begin with. During the first meeting you should lay a foundation for the actions you might take. Share why you came to the group, major turning points in your life (especially regarding gayness), the issues that move you strongly, what excites you and what scares you about direct action, and what kinds of actions you are prepared to take. After you have developed knowledge of each other and trust in the group, choose a focus for action. Plan an action which is small enough for your group to handle but which could be repeated or expanded into a campaign involving others.

Next, prepare yourselves for the event. Role-play how you will respond to hecklers, curious bystanders, provocateurs, sympathizers, the police and the press. Role-play the demonstration itself. Briefly state the key point(s) you want to make to the public; use these in your press releases, publicity, and signs and in all your interviews with the press. Get together before the demonstration begins so that each person can share how s/he feels and what support s/he needs from the group. Afterwards, evaluate the experience: How did you feel? Did it go as planned? What was accomplished? How could you do it better next time? Finally consider follow-up: What must still be done? How could you build on the successes of the demonstration? Is there energy to continue? Does the issue or the approach need to be altered?

Increasing our skills

Many concrete skills and much understanding, confidence, and intuition are required to create effective actions, organizations, and movements. As we work together we should take care to develop our skills and knowledge and to learn from each other.

Getting trained in political organizing, working in groups, and fighting oppression can increase our skills and effectiveness. MNS trainers in many parts of the U.S. (and sometimes in other parts of the world) can develop one-day or weekend workshops designed to meet the needs of specific groups for skills in planning strategy, organizing political action campaigns, changing oppressive dynamics, resolving conflict, and many other areas.[6]

Struggling against racism

By ourselves gays cannot win the war against heterosexism and the capitalist and patriarchal system of which it is a part. We therefore must identify and change our own oppressive attitudes and behaviors. White lesbians and gay men need to rid ourselves of racism in order that lesbians and gay men of color can have an equal part in shaping the movement.

Lesbians and gay men must ensure that the lesbian/gay movement itself grows in diversity and unity and that we cooperate with other oppressed groups. The national gay and lesbian march on Washington in October 1979 was a step in this direction. After an initial struggle, half the seats on the planning committee for the march were reserved for women. Money was set aside for minorities and women to travel to the march. And most important, the first Third World lesbian and gay conference was held in connection with the march. Audrey Lorde, in her keynote speech to the conference, said:

> This weekend we are here not only to share experience and connection, not only to discuss the many aspects of freedom for all homosexual peoples.... We are also here to examine our roles as powerful forces within our own communities. For not one of us will be free until we are all free, and until all members of our communities are free. So we are here to help shape a world where all people can flourish, beyond racism, beyond classism, and beyond homophobia.[7]

To shape such a world is the task of white as well as Third World gays, and of heterosexuals. We must each begin with ourselves and our own communities. Black lesbians and gay men need to challenge homophobia where we encounter it in Black communities and racism where we encounter it in lesbian/gay communities. White lesbians and gay men also need to challenge racism within the gay community and homophobia as well as racism within the white community. We each must identify and change *our own* oppressive attitudes and behaviors. Thus we make our movement open to all and we become solid allies of other liberation movements. Specifically, white lesbians and gay men need to rid ourselves of racism so that we do not place obstacles in the way of Third World lesbians and gay men having an equal part in the lesbian/gay movement.

Ridding Ourselves of Racism: Advice by Whites to Whites

1. Explore how racism hurts us by robbing us of knowledge of, and friendship with, Third World people.

2. Seek out interactions and develop (more) friendships with Third World people, both gay and heterosexual. Each time we have a caring, honest (not patronizing or token) interaction with a person of color, it is a victory against racism.

3. Discover how we have been forced against our wills to participate in injustice and oppression, especially racism. For example, as children, were we forbidden to play with children of color or visit their homes?

4. Reclaim our personal strength to fight for justice. Because this strength was robbed from us when we were forced to participate in racism as children, it feels hard to stand up against racism now.

5. Interrupt racist remarks and jokes and point out how they are part of everyone's oppression.

6. Become aware of and eliminate less obvious (to us) racism in our own behavior and challenge it in others. Ask ourselves if we are taking people of color seriously or being patronizing or ingratiating.

7. Educate ourselves. A good place to start is by reading: *This Bridge Called My Back: Writings By Radical Women of Color*, edited by Cherrie Moraga and Gloria Anzaldua; *But Some of Us Are Brave: Black Women's Studies*, edited by Gloria T. Hull, Patricia Bell Scott, and Barbara Smith; *Top Ranking: A Collection of Articles on Racism and Classism in the Lesbian Community*, compiled by Joan Gibbs and Sara Bennett; *off our backs; a woman's news journal*, November 1979 (special issue on racism and sexism); *Conditions 5* (special issue of writings by Black women); *Blaming the Victim*, by William Ryan.[8]

8. Begin consciousness-raising groups, workshops, or task forces against racism within the lesbian/gay community.[9]

9. Don't assume that Third World gays' needs are identical to ours (nor that they are entirely different). Find out about these needs by including Third World gays in planning committees or, if this is not possible, by asking the advice of Third World activists.

10. Since being Third World in a primarily white organization is not easy, find out from lesbians and gay men of color in the organization what the problems are and commit the time and energy to make the necessary changes.

11. Include Third World speakers, poets, and musicians in public events and publicize these events to Third World as well as white lesbians and/or gay men.

12. Celebrate Third World cultures (music, food, language, customs) as well as our own cultures.

13. Include Third World gays when researching gay history.

14. Do not spend money at segregated gay establishments—demand that they be integrated.

15. Locate gay services in areas easily accessible to all people.

16. Organize gay contingents to participate in protests against repression of Third World peoples.

17. Organize anti-racist contingents in gay and lesbian marches.

In addition to the above, it is essential that whites listen to and learn from the experiences of Third World people in the movement. For this reason, we quote at length from Hope Landrine's article in *off our backs* on the racism and classism she experienced in the women's movement:

It appears to me that ingratiation and patronage are, by far, the most common modus operandi of feminist racism and feminist classism. . . . Ingratiation generally manifests itself in (a) exaggerated compliments given to minority and lower-class women any time we make a "feminist statement." This includes being told that we are "original," "brilliant," and "outstanding" any time we make a statement that is so classically feminist that it is really no more than rhetoric. (b) Being "shown-off" and "shown" as tokens to white feminists through unnecessary invitations to elitist conferences and affairs at which we may have nothing substantially unique to say, and having minor, clearly average prose pieces sent around the feminist community. (c) Feminist shuffling, grinning, and verbal pats on the head, accompanied by statements of the we're-so-happy-that-ONE-OF-YOU-could-make-it type. Verbal shuffling and ingratiating are always followed by *nonverbal* dominance behavior.

Patronage generally manifests itself in (a) frequent requests for the "minority" or "lower class" woman's point of view, based on the assumption that we are representatives of these women and that minority and poor women all share the same perspective (i.e., all alike), (b) avoidance of serious discussions with minority and poor women of feminist theory and strategy, based on the assumptions that we "really" aren't committed to the movement (other commitments), don't know the classic movement literature, or can only speak about minority and poor women's "issues," (c) an inclination toward avoiding criticism of, and disagreement with, minority and poor women, based on the assumption that we "don't know" any better or shouldn't be expected to (because of those "other" commitments), or out of a desire *not* to appear racist and classist. On this last example of feminist racism and classism I must add a personal experience about which I still chuckle. The patronage I experienced from white feminists in NYC was so overwhelming that once I decided to test it. One evening I planted myself at a table in the Women's Coffeehouse. Prior to, and after, the concert of that evening, I attempted to engage in several serious discussions of politics with a number of well known feminists (including the musician), none of whom know me. I began with a few serious, sensible, but controversial statements. The response was smiles and head-nodding. I went on to statements that were progressively more absurd. Still, no disagreement, but a few questions for clarification, and more smiles. Finally while being sure I *did not* appear insane, I made the most utterly absurd statements I could think of, and one statement that I knew one feminist disagreed with, since she had publicly indicated her disagreement. To my surprise her response was a smile, and *agreement*.[10]

A white activist has written:

> When I first realized how subtle white racism could be, I felt very awkward around Black people. I was constantly afraid I would make a mistake, and would patronize them or in some unconscious way show that I wasn't seeing them for who they are. But then I realized that I was so stiff and timid that I wasn't being me at all—and being shy around Blacks was another kind of racism!
>
> I started to think it was hopeless until I realized that none of this is really my fault and the point isn't to dance around the edges of living trying to be politically correct, but instead to be honest and real. Of course I'll make mistakes—doesn't everybody?—but I can't learn if I can't be me. So when I started to relax I found there was a better flow to things, and I could be more vulnerable. I knew things were happening when one Black friend told me, "I used to admire you but wondered if you were real. Now I see you get embarrassed and be human like everybody else."

Finally, the work of Third World lesbian and/or gay men's groups such as Salsa Soul Sisters (NYC) and Philadelphia Black Gays is an important part of our movement. Salsa Soul Sisters organizes workshops, publishes a newsletter, and holds weekly discussions attended by 30 to 50 Black, hispanic, and white lesbians. It has 200 members from all economic classes, ranging in age from 17 to 55.[11] Philadelphia Black Gays "seeks to strengthen the bond between women and men in the Third World sexual minorities community...and confronts sexism and racism, both in the gay community and in society at large. The goals of Philadelphia Black Gays also include communication with Black lesbians and gay men and with the heterosexual community, creating a financially strong community and creating local support systems for Third World sexual minority members."[12]

Struggling against classism

There is much work to be done to eliminate classism in the lesbian and gay men's movements.[13] The work has begun with consciousness raising, study groups, writing, fighting, organization-building and -breaking, and dialogue. These are the methods of growth that have been so important to the women's movement since the '60s; now gays are using them to build awareness of class issues. As a result, new things are happening that need to be continued and built on:

—Sliding fee scales that take into account class background and income differences are being used for events and services.
—Childcare at events is much more common.
—Movement people are challenging the assumption that all people have the time and income to volunteer for organizations and events.
—New ways of co-parenting, income-sharing, and pooling work are being developed.

—Movement people are challenging the assumption that people's backgrounds are middle-class and that middle-class behavior is desirable.
—Middle-class people are working to overcome their own intellectualism and competitiveness.[14]
—Working-class people are working to overcome their hopelessness and acceptance of a hard life.
—More people are recognizing that coming out means different things in different economic situations and are exploring ways to help everyone to survive.

One of the problems activists can run into regarding classism is a "heady," abstract way of looking at class. Some radicals turn Marxist analysis into yet another moralism, a set of categories dripping with judgment. Then, while idealizing the working class, they manage to keep the whole concept removed enough from people's experience so that "political" is divorced, once again, from "personal."

The Philadelphia section of Movement for a New Society tried an experiential approach to defining class. In a large room they brainstormed characteristics of their upbringings which seemed linked to class: family get-togethers or parties, trips to the local beach or to Europe, drinking from jelly glasses or from matching goblets, the city streets or summer camp, community college or Ivy League schools, sleeping with siblings or each child having a room, and so on. The group lumped together the characteristics that seemed to go together, then gathered in small groups according to which "lump" they belonged to. Some individuals had to visit several small groups, and uncovered the ambiguities of mixed class background. The small groups shared what growing up had been like and how it affected their view of the world and were excited to discover how important their class origin was to the way they looked at themselves and the world. People whose parents had disguised their class situation discovered for the first time that they were working-class. Upper-middle-class people found others who shared their guilt feelings, and began to move beyond guilt to a more solid basis for action.

A series of forums followed in which the experiential side of class was linked to societal analysis. Members of an ongoing working-class group gave each other support and challenged others in the network on classism, and upper-middle-class people met to consider their responsibility in redistributing wealth and unlearning their negative class patterns, while not putting themselves down as people. Although much of the initiative-taking leadership of MNS has come, from the start, from people of working-class backgrounds, there continued to be a need for support among working-class people for becoming more articulate; writing projects became important for that.

MNS has found value in "speak-outs" in which working-class people spend an evening telling others in the organization what it is like to experience the oppression of classism; members from other class backgrounds meet to help each other hear about oppression more clearly, and act on it. The annual network meeting and some of the training programs operate on an "ability to pay" basis; that is, the budget for the project is raised through voluntary contributions, taking class background and present circumstances into account. As people challenge and support each other in this process, not only is the needed money raised, but consciousness gets raised at the same time.

Lesbian and gay men's organizations need to encourage the formation of working-class caucuses where people can support each other's leadership skills and strengthen their working-class perspective. Spokespeople for lesbian/gay organizations should routinely include working-class people. Publications should be reviewed with an eye toward readability, dropping the needlessly academic words or specialized political language. A warm, open tone for organizational meetings should be set that will help everyone feel included. Working-class people (and members of other oppressed groups) may lack the confidence to make easy conversation with strangers and may need special efforts at community-building, such as introductions in small groups.[15]

After its annual convention, a national gay organization got some disappointed letters from people who were in isolated situations and had been looking forward to the warm fellowship of a gay community. Instead, they found that people who already knew each other seemed delighted to be together, and they found no comfortable way into the sociability of the convention.

The next year a group-process facilitator began the convention by leading everyone through a series of community-building exercises for an entire morning. The convention buzzed with excitement and positive energy, and the president heard for months afterward positive comments on how warmly accepted participants felt that year.

Struggling against ageism

Identity groups and speak-outs can help lesbian and gay organizations cut through the fog of stereotypes of age as well as of class and race. Often it is through a speak-out that people first become aware of how resourceful older people are and how wide their experience is—no one had thought to listen before, or even ask.

Individual gays can take responsibility to sit down with an older person and ask how things used to be; there are many rich life stories that are waiting to be shared, as the documentary film *Word Is Out* has shown. Life stories benefit not only the listener but also the story-teller; a good listener provides tremendous affirmation of the worth of an older person, in contradiction to society, which tends to ignore older people as being "over the hill" or "all washed up."

Lesbian and gay organizations can learn about the special needs of older and younger gays and incorporate them into demands for change. European gay organizations have made substantial gains in recent years in getting the age of consent for sex lowered. A particular problem for younger lesbians and gays is lack of access to bars, the most frequented of gay gathering places. Alternatives such as coffeehouses are particularly important for building unity across age lines.

A common problem for adults is remembering how intelligent children are. Since people talked down to us when we were young (including ridiculous baby talk when we were toddlers), we are likely to repeat the mistake. The intelligence of youngsters thrives on direct, human communication. They want information; honest and direct answers give them what they need and build a relationship of mutual respect.

Five-year-old Jennifer seemed intent on eating her breakfast, but suddenly addressed her father and his friend who had slept over the previous night. "Daddy, you and Roger are lovers, right?" "Yes," I replied. "Then," Jennifer continued, "why don't we call you a mommy and daddy?"

That started an explanation of love beyond traditional roles.

A month later Jennifer's friend Marion was eating dinner at our house. After the silent grace, Jennifer spoke up with what seemed to be the continuation of an argument she was having with Marion. "Daddy, isn't it true that men can make love with men and women can make love with women?" "Yes, that's true," I said. "You see?" Jennifer turned to Marion. "Men don't even need women to make love."

Marion hastened to cover her tracks. "I already knew that," she said. Jennifer turned back to me, with a puzzled expression. "How do men make love?" she said.

I started to describe gay male love-making while adults around the table, trying to look casual, dug into their beans. I didn't go on very long because Jennifer's curiosity was soon satisfied, and she launched into another topic.

Struggling against chemical dependency

Gay people become alcoholic and addicted out of all proportion to our numbers, partly because bars are our sanctuary and partly because of the multiple oppression many of us face—gay and female, gay and Black, gay and working-class, and so on. It is vital for gay people to understand the political significance of drug and alcohol use and begin to remove its influence from our lives. To stop or decrease one's use of potentially addictive substances can be a strong step towards personal liberation and can also help free one's energy and time for other, possibly more productive uses.

We have already outlined the patriarchy's reason for encouraging drug and alcohol use among oppressed peoples. Millions of dollars are spent each year in advertising alcoholic beverages and cigarettes, holding out the most attractive and desirable images as bait. In reality, the consumption of these substances costs our people an incredible amount, not only in cash but in human lives. Since the majority of those affected are working-class people, women, Blacks, young people, and other members of oppressed groups, and since their addiction contributes to their continued oppression, big business and government are unlikely to do anything about the gradually worsening situation.

We, however, can provide non-alcoholic alternatives at social gatherings or, better yet, announce ahead of time that a particular gathering is to be chemical-free. We can support chemical-free spaces in our communities: coffeehouses, discos, restaurants, gay community centers. We can challenge our own and friends' use of addictive substances. We can encourage activities that lend themselves to chemical-free socializing, such as discussion and consciousness-raising groups, softball and volleyball games. We should remember that recovering alcoholics and addicts are often invisible, in the same way gay people are often invisible, and should not pressure our friends and acquaintances to drink or use drugs. We should assume that people around us or close to us may be chemically dependent and moderate our use accordingly. If we know a recovering alcoholic or addict, we can refrain from using such substances in her or his presence as a gesture of support and solidarity.

When I was trying to quit drinking and smoking marijuana, I had an especially hard time at parties. It was difficult being the only person who wasn't high. At one potluck when I was feeling particularly down, my friend Michael came over to me and announced that, in support of my struggle to stop doing it, he wasn't going to smoke or drink that evening. I felt incredibly warm towards him; and as a result of my stand and his support, that particular group of people has cut its chemical intake substantially.

If we know other gay people who seem to be abusing drugs or alcohol, we can best help them by educating ourselves on the subject and then refusing to cooperate with their addictive behavior. If we refuse to drink with them or buy them drugs and if we tell them what we see them doing, we may eventually help them to stop hurting themselves this way. It is important to continue to appreciate the person while pointing out the destructiveness of the behavior.

Because society does not usually provide politically aware treatment for substance abusers, one big step gays can take is to organize gay-run treatment centers for those in our community who need such services. Los Angeles has such a center, as do San Francisco, Minneapolis and St.

Paul, and other cities. In doing this we must be careful not to reinforce the helpless-victim mentality that so many addicts develop. As we help people get in touch with their feelings of oppression, we can at the same time help them to develop the skills they need to break out of that oppression, whether that be assertiveness training, meditation or new job skills. This kind of support in our communities can be an important part of a strong grass-roots political movement for long-term social change.

Struggling for adequate health care

While it may not be possible to change the medical establishment completely, there are a number of things we as gay people can do to become more in charge of our treatment as health consumers.

The first and most important thing is to take care of our bodies as much as possible ourselves and to see medical treatment as the last resort rather than as the cure for all ills. If we accept the responsibility for our own health care, we approach the question from a position of personal power rather than as victims.

We can learn to be assertive with our health care providers. For example, a man who has had oral or anal sex with another man needs to ask to have these areas checked for VD. A woman who has a yeast infection may need to ask under what circumstances she can pass it on to a female lover. If a physician or other health professional refuses to pay attention to what we are saying about our health, then we have every right to seek medical treatment elsewhere.

If a physician seems open to you as a gay person but lacking in information, be prepared to recommend some reading material. Don Clarke's *Loving Someone Gay* is good, as is *Lesbian/Woman* by Del Martin and Phyllis Lyons, or *Society and the Healthy Homosexual*, by George Weinberg.[16]

Under the Freedom of Information Act (as of this writing) we have the right to examine files that are kept on us, including medical files. If negative remarks have been made about our gayness by physicians or psychiatrists, we have the right to request that they be removed and, if they refuse to do so, to ask that the records be transferred to a health professional who is more aware of the potential abuse of such remarks.

When I came out to my doctor, he was surprised but not negative. The next time I went to see him, I noticed that he had entered a progress note in my medical file to the effect that I was a lesbian. I pointed this out and asked him to remove it, explaining that I felt the information might someday be used against me. He quickly agreed with me and erased the entry.

We have a right to the best health care available; if we cannot get it in established institutions, we must consider building alternatives of our own. Many cities' gay centers now include VD clinics, counseling services and treatment for drug and alcohol abuse. There are large number of gays in the medical, nursing, and other health-related professions. Those professionals among us who are still in closets can be supportive of openly gay health professionals and can seriously consider coming out ourselves. We can also be supportive of gay patients who are often separated from their lovers by hospital rules and regulations about next-of-kin. Those of us who are in a position to do so can pressure the establishment to change such rules, do educational public speaking to other health professionals, and challenge the assumptions made by the establishment that everyone is heterosexual.

It may feel to gay health professionals that we have a lot to lose by coming out of the closet. In reality it is the other way around, because if we continue to be silent about the misuse of power in the medical establishment, we contribute to our own oppression as well as to that of our gay sisters and brothers.

Struggling against violence

As we reach toward androgyny, women and men find themselves coming from very different places on the issue of violence. Most women have been socialized to avoid physical fighting and even verbal conflict; they have been conditioned to be "nice" and to defer to others with stronger wills (i.e., men). As they move away from their habitual passivity and try, with much fear, to find that posture called "assertiveness," they may waver back and forth between hostile aggressiveness and sullen surrender. In Aikido there is something called the "ki." It is the center, the focus of poise, the confident and relaxed and alert attention which each of us has within—sometimes to our surprise!

Flow and I were sitting down to plan a meeting of Women Against Violence Against Women (ironically enough), when Lynn came in the front door—scared. She said, "A woman is getting beat up down the street." We stood up and said, "Come on—let's go."

We heard children screaming and people yelling in the doorway of a house; a man was trying to push his way in and beating on a woman who was yelling at him to stay out of her house and her life. When we ran up onto the porch he stopped and addressed us coldly: "May I help you?" I said, "We heard someone was getting beat up." He replied, "Mind your own goddamn business!" shoved the woman inside the house, and slammed the door shut against us. We paused, and then Flow opened the door and walked in, and I followed close behind.

We went into the room where he was still shoving her around, and Flow called to her, "Do you need help? Do you want us to be here?" The woman was crying real hard, and didn't answer, but her cousin, who was there also, told us to stay. The man came over to us then, aggressive and furious, and asked, "So what are you, the police?"

Flow replied calmly, "We're women who care about other women who're getting hurt." "So what are you, lesbians?" he demanded. Flow replied, still unaggressively, "We are women . . . who care about other women."

He began to shove Flow around a bit and she was sliding a little, in her stocking feet. I went up behind him and firmly but gently grasped him by the upper arms and pulled him away from her. He wheeled around to me and sneered, "And what do you think you're doing?" I answered calmly, "I'm holding you back from pushing my friend around." He tried to push me around some then but I was in my bare feet and knew how to hold my ground solidly, having recently taken a self-defense class. I kept my face an impassive mask, and held his eyes steadily as he tried to intimidate me. He turned back to yell and push Flow around then, but she had taken her socks off and stood firmly now too. For a brief moment she almost let her anger out at him, which was what his macho-violent mood was waiting for to trigger a real attack. Instead she took a deep breath and returned to a firm undefensive stare. His face went kind of blank and then he swaggered half-heartedly out the front door, still muttering threats.[17]

These women, in an emergency situation, found strongly assertive and nonviolent means of stopping a beating. A self-defense course was part of their preparation for that moment, as well as the confidence which grows from taking action with sisters against patriarchy.[18]

Most men have been socialized to value violence and even to use it; in most circles violence (which includes non-physical bureaucratic ruthlessness) is the proof of masculinity.[19]

In reaching for androgyny, therefore, most men need to get in touch with their gentleness, their intelligent concern for the needs of others, their ability to resist rather than overpower. Men need to find a new center of strength which is flexible and responsive like a willow tree rather than rigid and unassailable like a rock. The new strength of an androgynous man is enduring rather than explosive; it proceeds from self-knowledge (including awareness of fear) rather than denial of feeling.

In order to move past the old conditioning about violence to find new, androgynous ways to wage conflict, lesbians and gay men can organize workshops in which they role-play conflict situations, experimenting with tactics while working through feelings. They can also form study groups to learn about the practice of nonviolent action, a means of struggle which we believe is the most non-sexist form developed so far. Patriarchal culture has generally been uneasy with nonviolent struggle, and we believe with good reason: it *is* subversive of the sex-role division which keeps patriarchy in place! It is no accident therefore that women taking strong roles in direct-action campaigns have had their sexuality questioned and that nonviolent men have for years been hassled as "fairies."

WE CAN MAKE THE CHANGES   143

Becoming powerful

Both gays and our non-gay allies need to see the dynamic at work and support each other in moving out of oppression. First, there is awareness of victimization. When that awareness comes to a lesbian or gay man, it may come hard, with anger and self-pity. We may accuse our non-gay friends of withdrawing from us or ignoring us, and then create opportunities for them to do so. We may hopelessly accept fear or unhappiness because "I'm so oppressed I can't be happy or unafraid." We may seek therapy which focuses on how much we hurt and how we can be "happy" like everyone else—better job, new house, gay marriage. We may try to join the mainstream—or lash out sporadically while huddling under the covers. We may remain angry at other oppressed people when, because of the anti-gay conditioning they have also received, they act badly toward us. We may assume that other gays are "too oppressed" or "hurting too badly" to stand up with us in the struggle for liberation. Our strategies for change may center on feeling better in society as it is, or escaping—not on making revolution.

All these reactions can be seen among lesbians and gay men, and in a sense they are natural. They are, however, the reactions of victims, not of powerful people who are taking charge of their situation. These reactions, therefore, are best seen as a stage, a place of transition from which we need to move to recover our full humanity.

The empowerment stage comes as we expect ourselves to remake our environments into the liberated zones that we deserve. We must expect ourselves to act powerfully—and our non-gay allies should expect it of us. It is no favor to oppressed people to play along with their victim behavior. We do not need pity, or even sympathy. Of course it will take a lot of time and effort to remake our environment on the largest scale. However, small-scale changes are the foundation from which large-scale changes will grow.

When I was on the staff of a summer camp, I was troubled by the frequent use of "faggot," "gay," and "girl" as put-down words among the boys. Some counselors tried to stop the practice by confronting individual boys, but the problem was too great to deal with on a one-to-one basis.

Finally we decided to take on everyone at once in an all-camp evening gathering. The program started with "There's Room for Everyone in This World," a song from the movie "Pete's Dragon." Next, a counselor explained the purpose of the program and defined the words (some of the eight- and nine-year-olds didn't know what "faggot" meant, even though they used it).

Another counselor spoke on how it hurt her as a heterosexual to hear anti-gay language used. I stood up and explained how it hurt me as a gay man to know it was happening. A twelve-year-old boy we had talked with earlier then got up and said that he, as a Black, had been called "nigger" sometimes outside of camp and figured that anti-gay name-calling was probably just as hurtful. Two thirteen-year-old girls were next: they explained that they like to cuddle and touch each other, but that they got hassled for that in their school and were called "lesbians" in a sneering way. They said they didn't want to have to worry about that at camp.

We threw the discussion open at that point. Several campers and a couple of counselors spoke about not wanting name-calling to continue.Then the thirteen-year-old leader of the boys offered a moving confession that he now realized it was wrong but he was so used to calling "faggot" that it would be hard to stop; he would try, however, and hoped people would forgive a slip now and then. We ended the program with a song.

Anti-gay name-calling disappeared at the camp. When new campers came and started doing it (since it is common everywhere), the experienced campers immediately let the newcomers know that it wasn't tolerated at the camp. For the rest of the summer we could all breathe the fresh air in more ways than one.

We can insist that our friends, gay and non-gay, stand by us in oppressive situations. We can create a life-style and build a community which can help us to be happy and unafraid and support us in changing society.

There is power in *expecting*—in expecting that the allies will be there, and that we can be assertive. Of course there will be disappointments. Being our whole selves in the present, refusing to hold back any longer, is itself a victory even if the results of a particular act are sometimes meager. And, as more of us realize we have power, enlist allies, and boldly stand up against all injustice, we will experience more fully the act of liberation. We will be living, in all its outrageousness, the human revolution.

> *Take heart, all those in the struggle*
> *Our lives are where it begins*
> *So celebrate through the hard times,*
> *For we will win.*[20]

Notes

Most of the books and records mentioned here should be available at your local gay bookstore. If not, write to Giovanni's Room, 345 S. 12th St., Philadelphia, PA 19107.
• These and other resources are available from Movement for a New Society, 4722 Baltimore Ave., Philadelphia, PA 19143.

1. The continental European scene, especially Germany, is described by John Lauritsen and David Thorstad in *The Early Homosexual Rights Movement (1864-1935)* (New York: Times Change Press, 1974). For Britain, see Jeffrey Weeks, *Coming Out: Homosexual Politics in Britain, from the Nineteenth Century to the Present* (London and New York: Quartet Books, 1977). For the U.S., see Jonathan Katz, *Gay American History: Lesbians and Gay Men in the U.S.A., A Documentary* (New York: Crowell, 1976; Avon/Discus, 1978).

2. See Heinz Heger's history of the Nazi attempt to exterminate gays, *The Men with the Pink Triangle* (Boston: Alyson Pub., 1980).

3. John D'Emiolio describes this period in his series of articles for *Body Politic* (Toronto). The articles are based on his Ph.D. dissertation on gay history. The series called "Dreams Deferred," appeared in issues 48-50, Nov. 1978-Feb. 1979: Part 1, "Radical Beginnings," Part 2, "Public Actions, Private Fears," Part 3, "Reaction, Redbaiting and Respectability."

4. An autobiographical account of one woman's coming out in the context of social change work in the '60s and '70s is found in the interview with Leslie Cagan in Dick Cluster, ed., *They Should Have Served that Cup of Coffee* (Boston: South End Press, 1979).

5. Richard Goldstein, "The Future of Gay Liberation: Sex on Parole," *Village Voice*, 20-26 Aug. 1980, p. 21.

6. More readers learned of some of the main points of that draft through Marc Killinger's article-review, "Lesbian and Gay Liberation in the '80s: Androgyny, Men, and Power," in *Working Papers on Gay/Lesbian Liberation and Socialism* (Chicago: New American Movement, 1979), and in Pam Mitchell, ed., *Pink Triangles: Radical Perspectives on Gay Liberation* (Boston: Alyson Pub., 1980). Marc's critical feedback was helpful in our revision.

Chapter I

1. For an excellent analysis of the New Right's use of anti-gay and anti-feminist feeling, and the Left's inadequate response, see Linda Gordon and Allen Hunter, "Sex, Family, and the New Right: Anti-Feminism as a Political Force."

2. Del Martin and Phyllis Lyon, *Lesbian/Woman* (New York: Bantam, 1972), p. 110.

3. Same as above, p. 111.

4. Letter from the National Gay Task Force, Nov. 1980.

5. A moving and revealing description of what this feels like from the "inside" is by Malcolm Boyd, *Take Off the Masks* (Garden City, NY: Doubleday, 1978).

6. Mike Silverstein in *Out of the Closets: Voices of Gay Liberation* edited by Allen Young and Karla Jay (New York: Pyramid Books, 1974), p. 168.

7. City Hall protest reported in Gunter David, "Gay Rightists Fight Police," *The Philadelphia Evening Bulletin*, 4 December 1975, pp. 1-E, 5-E. Stairs incident from personal conversation with Sharon Owens, member of Dyketactics.

8. A review of the studies is in Mark Freedman, *Homosexuality and Psychological Functioning* (Belmont, CA: Brooks/Cole Publishing Co., 1971).

9. Gerald C. Davison and John M. Neale, *Abnormal Psychology: An Experimental Clinical Approach*, 3rd ed. (New York: John H. Wile & Sons, Inc., 1982), pp. 363-364.

10. Radicalesbians Health Collective in *Out of the Closets*, noted above, p. 134.

11. Same as above, p. 122.

12. Boston Women's Health Book Collective, *Our Bodies, Ourselves* (New York: Simon and Schuster, 1979), p. 63.

13. See Mitchell, ed., *Pink Triangles*, noted above, especially the article by the Los Angeles Research Group, "Toward a Scientific Analysis of the Gay Question," pp. 117-135.

14. Jill Johnston, *Lesbian Nation* (New York: Touchstone/Simon and Schuster, 1973), p. 68.

15. Radclyffe Hall, *The Well of Loneliness* (New York: Covici, 1928; Simon and Schuster, 1975).

Chapter II

1. Rita Mae Brown, *Rubyfruit Jungle* (Plainfield, VT: Daughters, Inc., 1973), p. 115.

2. Irene Schram, "Woman Becoming," *Amazon Quarterly*, Vol. 3, No. 1 (Nov. 1974), pp. 51-52.

3. Same as above.

4. Third World Gay Revolution (Chicago) and Gay Liberation Front (Chicago), "Gay Revolution and Sex Roles," in Silverstein, *Out of the Closets*, noted above, p. 257.

5. Gary Alinder, "My Gay Soul," in Silverstein, *Out of the Closets*, noted above, p. 283.

6. Bruce Kokopeli and George Lakey, "More Power Than We Want: Masculine Sexuality and Violence," in *Off Their Backs* (Philadelphia: New Society Publishers, 1983).*

7. Same as above.

8. Mike Silverstein, "The Politics of My Sex Life," in Silverstein, *Out of the Closets*, noted above, p. 271.

9. Third World Gay Revolution (Chicago) and others, in Silverstein, *Out of the Closets*, noted above, p. 252.

10. Silverstein, *Out of the Closets*, noted above, p. 272.

11. Ti-Grace Atkinson, "Lesbianism and Feminism," in Phyllis Berkly and others, eds., *Amazon Expedition* (Washington, NJ: Times Change Press, 1973) p. 11.

12. Joseph Pleck and Jack Sawyer, eds., *Men and Masculinity* (Englewood Cliffs, NJ: Prentice-Hall, 1974), p. 136.

13. Virginia Woolf's famous essay *Three Guineas* (New York: Harcourt, Brace/ Harbinger, 1938) traces connections between militarism and the oppression of women. She was part of the Bloomsbury Group of intellectuals who concerned themselves with literature, social reform, feminism, and pacifism.

14. Eugene C. Bianchi and Rosemary Radford Ruether, *From Machismo to Mutuality: Essays on Sexism and Woman-Man Liberation* (New York: Paulist Press, 1976), Chapter 3.

15. The power of the owners in both economics and politics is described more thoroughly in *Moving Toward a New Society*, by Susanne Gowan, George Lakey, William Moyer, and Richard Taylor. (Philadelphia: New Society Press, 1976).*

16. U.S. Department of Labor Statistics, "Employment status of black workers by sex and age" in *Employment and Earnings, January 1976* (Washington, D.C. Vol. 29. no. 1) p. 153.

17. Same as above, p. 179.

18. Goldstein, "Future of Gay Liberation," p. 21.

19. Richard Sennett and Jonathan Cobb show in their book *The Hidden Injuries of Class* (New York: Vintage, 1973) that working-class people already must struggle against loss of self-respect in this society. Add to that the impact of homophobia and one begins to see how the cards are stacked against working-class lesbians and gay men.

20. George, in Casey Adair and Nancy Adair, *Word Is Out* (New York: Dell, 1978), p. 75.

Chapter III

1. Anthropologist Ashley Montagu pulls together evidence that touching is essential for full health—for adults as well as children—in his book *Touching: The Human Significance of the Skin* (New York: Harper & Row's Perennial Library, 1972).

2. We hope the reader will see that our approach to androgyny is not the person-liberation-in-a-vacuum approach rightfully challenged by some feminist writers. Judith Long Laws, in her book *The Second X: Sex Role and Social Role*, refers to "most treatments of this concept [which] lack an analysis of the current situation and a plan for social change," and therefore become a "voguish pie-in-the-sky idea." (New York: Elsevier, 1979), p. 380.

We assume that babies are born androgynous and, if they grew up in a vacuum, would remain so. There is, of course, no vacuum; each society adopts certain values and socializes children into them through the lifting up of character ideals which reflect these values. Each society—including the liberated society we are working for—must answer the question: How shall I be when I grow up? The answer may provide a narrow range of behaviors linked, for example, to sex, or a broad range. Our envisioned society will not answer the quest by saying, Androgynous, since that concept grows out of an historical period when behaviors are polarized into masculine/feminine. Adults would not say Androgynous to young people, but an historically informed observer would notice that this new culture does, indeed, permit the flourishing of the androgynous human being.

3. Sheila Rowbotham has pointed out that major thinkers who were wise about the range of human cultures, like Margaret Mead, Ruth Benedict, and Sigmund Freud, have been unable to describe the essence of "woman." Their wish to counter oppression and let women emerge meant, in the patriarchal social context, letting women become masculinized, since "fully human" has been defined as "manlike." That is clearly inadequate; Freud shrank from the thought of losing feminine characteristics which provide a refuge from the hard cruel world (without, unfortunately, criticizing the hard cruel world of capitalism). Mead and Benedict had no wish to say women are the same as men in their essence, and in their studies as well as in their lives, these anthropologists were concerned with discovering the desirable and mysterious essence which transcends culture. The essence which transcends the cultures of sex roles is *completeness*, wholeness—the chance for a woman (or man) to express the whole range of human characteristics according to her unique individuality. Androgyny makes likely the woman-identified-woman, who is complete in herself (having access to all human characteristics) and loves herself so much that she is at home with her sex (individually and collectively).

Rowbotham describes the problem in *Woman's Consciousness, Man's World* (Baltimore: Penguin Books, 1973), pp. 7-9.

For a study of androgynous themes in western literaure, interesting even though it dodges the issue of gayness, see Carolyn G. Heilbrun, *Toward a Recognition of Androgyny* (New York: Harper Colophon Books, 1974).

4. For more on this aspect of Marxism, see Sheila Rowbotham, *Women, Resistance, and Revolution,* and Batya Weinbaum, *The Curious Courtship of Women's Liberation and Socialism* (Boston: South End Press, 1978). There has also been a socialist tradition which valued new life styles; in late nineteenth century England, Edward Carpenter combined gayness, socialism, feminism, simplicity of life, the value of manual labor, and spiritual growth. See Sheila Rowbotham and Jeffrey Weeks, *Socialism and the New Life: The Personal and Sexual Politics of Edward Carpenter and Havelock Ellis* (London: Pluto Press, 1977).

5. For a more developed sketch of new political and economic ideas, see Gowan and others, *Moving Toward a New Society,* noted above.

6. Nonviolent means of struggle also are described in Gowan and others, *Moving Toward a New Society,* noted above, Chapter 12.*

7. Sociologist Elise Boulding finds an historical basis for the tendency of women to prefer nonviolent means of waging conflict in their need, in many ticklish situations where they were not in a position to "call out the troops," nevertheless to take a stand and make it stick. Thus they developed skills that men who had easy access to violence did not develop. See her books *Women in the Twentieth Century World* (Beverly Hills: Sage Publications; New York: distributed by Halsted Press, 1977) and *The Underside of History: A View of Women through Time* (Boulder, CO: Westview Press, 1976).

Sociologist Gene Sharp in his book *Social Power and Political Freedom* (Boston: Porter Sargent, 1980) shows how strongly the chances for liberation are affected by the means people choose for struggle.

8. Marge Piercy, in her book *Woman on the Edge of Time* (New York: Fawcett, 1976), describes a society in which art flourishes, is highly participative, and reflects

a variety of cultural backgrounds. It is a pluralist vision of new societies, with institutions much like those we suggest, and embracing an androgynous character ideal.

Chapter IV

1. See George Lakey, *Strategy for a Living Revolution* (San Francisco: W.H. Freeman, 1973).*

2. This five-stage framework has been used by other writers to aid strategic thinking. Dancer Louise Bruyn's article "Theatre for a Living Revolution" (*Theaterwork*, Nov./ Dec. 1980) describes the role of people's theater and allied arts in the five stages. Her article is also in Severyn T.Bruyn and Paula M. Rayman, eds., *Non-Violent Action and Social Change* (Boston: Irvington Publishers, 1979).

3. Some fresh thinking in the Marxist tradition places value on what is called "prefigurative organizaton"—that is, organizing today in a way which includes some of the values of—or prefigures—the new society. See Carl Boggs, "Marxism, Prefigurative Communism, and the Problem of Workers' Control," *Radical America*, Vol. 11, No. 6 and Vol. 12, No. 1 (Nov. 1977-Feb. 1978), pp. 99-123.

4. See *Building Social Change Communities*, by the Training/Action Affinity Group of Movement for a New Society, 1979.*

5. See "Spinning the Web: Networks for Social Change, " by Peter Woodrow, in *Building Social Change Communities*, noted above.

6. Minutes of the South East Lesbian Network Meeting, 20 Jan., 1979. P.O. Box 120252, Nashville, TN 37212.

7. For information on the conferences and the network, write Lavender Left Network, P.O. Box 412, Village Station, New York, NY, 10014.

8. Richard K. Taylor, *Blockade* (Maryknoll, NY: Orbis Books, 1977).*

9. Michael Ward and Mark Freedman, "Defending Gay Rights: The Campaign Against the Briggs Initiative in California," *Radical America*, Vol. 3, No. 4, p. 12.

10. Same as above, p. 14.

11. An excellent book on the dynamics of confrontation and mass noncooperation is by Frances Fox Piven and Richard A. Cloward, *Poor People's Movements: Why They Succeed, How They Fail* (New York: Vintage, 1979). They emphasize the smart use of the right historical moment.

12. Amber Hollibaugh, interview in *Socialist Review*, May/June, 1979, cited in Ward and Freedman, *Radical America*, noted above, p. 20.

13. For case studies, see Chapter II of Lakey, *Strategy*, noted above.

14. We believe a revolutionary situation will arise for reasons given in Gowan and others, *Moving Toward a New Society*, noted above.*

Chapter V

1. For more discussion of the European witch burnings see *Gyn/Ecology: the Metaethics of Radical Feminism*, by Mary Daly (Boston: Beacon Press, 1978); *Witches, Midwives and Nurses: A History of Women Healers*, by Barbara Ehrenreich and Deirdre English (The Feminist Press, 1973); and *Woman Hating*, by Andrea Dworkin (Dutton, 1974).

2. Holly Near, on record album "Imagine My Surprise" (P.O. Box 996, Ukiah, CA: Redwood Records, 1978).

3. Rita Mae Brown, speech in Philadelphia, 1977.

4. Judy Lashof, "Pleiades: The Story of a Lesbian Communal House," *Communities Magazine*, July/Aug. 1977. This article is available by writing to Box 426, Louisa, VA 23093.

5. Rita Mae Brown, speech in Philadelphia, 1977.

6. Betsy Rose, "Don't Shut My Sister Out," record album "Sweet Sorcery" (with Cathy Winter), 1980. (Origami Records, P.O. Box 8012, Albany, NY 12203).

Chapter VI

1. To learn about the growing network of rural gays, one can subscribe to the periodical *RFD* (Rt. 1, Box 92E, Efland, NC 27243, $2/copy).

2. Two recent accounts of the gay men's world in the U.S. are Seymour Kleinberg, *Alienated Affections: Being Gay in America* (New York: St. Martin's Press, 1980) and Edmund White, *States of Desire: Travels in Gay America* (New York: E.P. Dutton, 1980).

3. George, in Adair, *Word Is Out*, noted above, pp. 72-73.

4. Martin S. Weinberg and Colin J. Williams, *Male Homosexuals* (New York: Penguin Books, 1975), p. 286.

5. Same as above, p. 281.

6. Same as above, p. 284.

7. Because this playful way of looking at the world has an obvious affinity to theater, people often mistakenly assume that the theater must be a liberated zone for gays. There is more space for gays in theater than in some areas of society, but there has also been enforced closetry as well as homophobic stereotypes in the plays and films themselves. See William M. Hoffman's introduction to his collection, *Gay Plays* (New York: Avon/Bard Books, 1979).

8. Ralph Schaffer, *Out of the Closets*, noted above, p. 278.

9. Same as above, p. 311.

10. Gene Sharp, *Politics and Nonviolent Action* (Boston: Porter Sargent, 1973).

11. Susan Brownmiller, *Against Our Will: Men, Women and Rape* (New York: Simon and Schuster, 1975).

12. A sympathetic and clear article describing the dynamics of S & M is by Ian Young, "Sado-Masochism," in Len Richmond and Gary Noguera, eds., *The New Gay Liberation Book* (Palo Alto: Ramparts Press, 1979), pp. 45-53.

13. Mark, in Adair, *Word is Out*, noted above, p. 120.

14. For practical ways to encourage good process in organization, see Virginia Coover and others. *Resource Manual for a Living Revolution* (Philadelphia: New Society Press, 1977).

15. Masters and Johnson, *Homosexuality in Perspective* (Waltham, MA: Little, Brown, 1979).

16. Jack Nichols writes about the butch theme in gay male culture in "Butcher Than Thou: Beyond Machismo" in Richmond, *New Gay Liberation*, noted above.

17. Two aticles which helpfully interpret the development of fairy gatherings, both personally and politically, are by Don Collier and John P. Ward, "Who Are the Radical Fairies? Two Perspectives," in *Gay Community News*, Nov. 22, 1980, pp. 8.

18. Weinberg, *Male Homosexuals*, noted above, p. 212-213.

19. Tede in Adair, *Word Is Out*, noted above, p. 87.

20. For suggestions on how to conduct a clearness session, see Peter Woodrow's pamphlet, *Clearness: Processes for Supporting Individuals and Groups in Decision-Making*, 1979. •

21. An amazingly frank account of their bisexual marriage is by Barry Kohn and Alice Matusow, *Barry and Alice* (Englewood Cliffs, NJ: Prentice-Hall, 1980).

22. The poignancy of gay fathers separated from their children is revealed by Mary Mendola, who found that 33 percent of the gay fathers in her study did not see their children at all! Mary Mendola, *The Mendola Report: A New Look At Gay Couples* (New York: Crown Publishers, 1980), pp. 84-86.

23. Charlie Murphy, "Walls to Roses: Songs of Changing Men" (Folkways Records, 1979). This record is available from MNS, 4722 Baltimore Ave., Phila., PA 19143.

Chapter VII

1. See Chapter V, "African Genital Mutilation: The Unspeakable Atrocities," in Daly, *Gyn/Ecology*, noted above; pp. 153-177.

2. An excellent book that gives suggestions to women on how to explore masturbation from this perspective is *Liberating Masturbation*, by Betty Dodson (New York: Bodysex Designs, 1974).

3. See Ruth Baetz, *Lesbian Crossroads* (New York: William Morrow & Co., 1980) and Julia Penelope Stanley and Susan J. Wolfe, *The Coming Out Stories* (Watertown, MA: Persephone Press, 1981).

4. Charlie Murphy, "Catch the Fire," Good Fairy Productions, P.O. Box 12188, Broadway Station, Seattle, WA 98102. Another example of a gay men's record with a feminist consciousness is Tom Wilson, "Gay Name Game," Aboveground Records.

5. *Study and Action for a New Society*, by the Philadelphia Macroanalysis Collective of the Movement for a New Society (Philadelphia: New Society Publishers, 1981), presents tools and processes useful to these study groups (although itself focusing on a general radical critique of society). The *Resource Manual for a Living Revolution*, noted above, also contains many useful tools and processes. •

6. For more information, write: Movement for a New Society, 4722 Baltimore Ave., Phila., PA 19143.

7. Audrey Lorde, "When Will the Ignorance End?" *Off Our Backs*, Nov. 1979, p. 8.

8. William Ryan, *Blaming the Victim* (New York: Vintage Books, 1976); *This Bridge Called My Back: Writings by Radical Women of Color*, edited by Cherrie Moraga and Gloria Anzaldua, (Watertown, MA: Persephone Press, 1981); *All the Women Are White, All the Blacks Are Men, But Some of Us Are Brave: Black Women's Studies*, edited by Gloria T. Hull, Patricia Bell Scott, and Barbara Smith (Old Westbury, NY: The Feminist Press, 1981); *Top Ranking: A Collection of Articles on Racism and Classism in the Lesbian Community*, compiled by Joan Gibbs and Sara Bennett, (New York: February 3rd Press, c/o Joan Gibbs and Sara Bennett, 306 Lafayette Avenue, Brooklyn, New York 11238, 1980).

It is interesting to note that to our knowledge most of the work by gays on racism is coming out of the feminist movement. This is not because there is more racism there than there is in the gay male movement, but because there is presently greater attention to and work being done on racism by the women's community. This is to be commended. We hope the gay men's movement will begin to address racism with this same fervor.

9. For consciousness-raising guidelines see *Off Our Backs*, Nov. 1979, p. 9. For a report on a series of four workshops on White Racism for Lesbians, write Sisterspace Education Committee, c/o The Christian Association, 3601 Locust Walk, Phila., PA 19104. For workshop ideas see Judy Katz, *White Awareness: A Manual for Anti-racism Training* (Norman, OK: University of Oklahoma Press, 1978).

10. Hope Landrine, "Culture, Feminist Racism and Feminist Classism: Blaming the Victim" *Off Our Backs*, Nov. 1979, p. 3.

11. Ann Allen Shockley, "The Salsa Soul Sisters," *Off Our Backs*, Nov. 1979, p. 13.

12. Statement of Philadelphia Black Gays, c/o Eromin Center, 1735 Naudain St., Phila., PA 19146.

13. Rita Mae Brown reminds us how important class is to women: "While material changes in child care, abortion, etc., would provide breathing space for women, we must recognize that they will not seriously alter the class divisions among women. These changes, if they come to pass, could not seriously challenge upper-class and middle-class women's control over lower-class women. Just because the control may be indirect—through husbands, fathers, brother—does not lessen its sting if you happen to be on the receiving end."—*A Plain Brown Rapper* (Oakland, CA: Diana Press, 1976) pp. 183-84.

14. By "intellectualism" we mean throwing around obscure and confusing names and concepts to enhance status or win arguments rather than to shed light. We value highly the good uses of the intellect.

"Many middle-class women, fearing that intellect will be mistaken for middle-class behavior and remembering *their* college experience, bury their brains in a morass of 'vibes,' 'gut feelings,' and outright hysteria. This is dogmatically declared 'true woman' behavior since men don't express their feelings. Serious organizing to end our oppression is suspect, ideological struggle is heresy; feelings are the way, the light and the truth—even when they result in political stagnation. Such an idea spells death to real political change if people cling to it."—Brown, *Rapper*, noted above, p. 103.

15. Specific techniques for building community feeling in your group can be found in Coover, *Resource Manual*, noted above.

16. Del Martin and Phyllis Lyon, *Lesbian/Woman* (New York: Bantam, 1972); Don Clark, *Loving Someone Gay* (Millbrae, CA: Celestial Arts, 1977, also available in Signet Classic paperback, NAL); George Weinberg, *Society and the Healthy Homosexual* (Garden City, NY: Anchor, 1973).

17. An excerpt from *Whose Hand is This? I Found It on My Ass and Other Tales of Resistance* (pamphlet), available from P.O. Box 7014, Minneapolis, MN 55407.

18. See *WIN* Magazine issue on Rape Resistance, 26 Apr. 1979.

19. See Kokopeli, "More Power Than We Want: Masculine Sexuality and Violence," noted above.

20. P.J. Hoffman, "We Will Make the Changes," on his record album "Muscle and Brain". *

About the Authors

Judy Lashof graduated from the University of Michigan, came out, and moved to Philadelphia in 1974. She has been speaking, writing and organizing as a lesbian feminist for over eight years. She has devoted considerable energy to promoting gay liberation within and through Movement for a New Society and Re-evaluation Counseling. Her innumerable contributions to the feminist movement include serving as a coordinator of the Free Women's School, of Women United to Take Back the Night and of Feminists Insist on Safe Transit (FIST). She earns her living teaching adults and recently returned to school to pursue a Master's Degree in Adult Literacy. Phoenix, a women's communal house in Philadelphia, is her home.

George Lakey is an activist, author, and teacher who is presently coordinating the Jobs with Peace Campaign in Philadelphia. He has lectured and led training workshops in ten European countries and New Zealand, and taught at the University of Pennsylvania, Haverford College, and the Martin Luther King, Jr., School of Social Change. He has led workshops for the Gay Activist Alliance, Integrity, and other gay organizations and was a founder of Men Against Patriarchy. He is revising his 1973 book *Strategy for a Living Revolution*, which will be republished by New Society Publishers.

Erika Thorne is developing a lesbian dance movement in Minneapolis. She has been through many changes, personal and political, since co-authoring this book. If she were writing now she would be more influenced by lesbian separatist politics, though she still cherishes the vision of a world where we all live together successfully.

Gerre Goodman moved from Tucson, Arizona, to Berkeley, California, to take a well-deserved sabbatical after ten years of non-stop political work which included everything fom guerrilla theater to a presentation for the Congressional hearings for the Peace Academy. She is currently examining her involvement with MNS and the radical left as they relate to her increasing commitment to the Jewish feminist community, her work with children, and especially her art. Gerre's visions include an ongoing involvement with both personal and community politics, and living simply but comfortably in a loving, nonviolent environment with other people's children, cats and a studio with good afternoon light.

new society publishers

RESOURCE MANUAL FOR A LIVING REVOLUTION

by Virginia Coover, Ellen Deacon, Charles Esser and Christopher Moore

The practical tools you need for everything from consciousness raising, working in groups, and developing communities of support to education, training, and organizing skills. Used by women's groups, disarmament and antinuclear activists, and community organizers worldwide. 25,000 copies in print. An activist's dream!

330 pages. Agendas. Exercises. New edition. 1981. ISBN (hardbound): 0-86571-015-5 $19.95 ISBN (paperback): 0-86571-008-2 $7.95

A MANUAL ON NONVIOLENCE AND CHILDREN

edited by Stephanie Judson

A new society starts with children! Help create an atmosphere where children and adults can resolve problems and conflicts nonviolently. Includes, *For the Fun of it! Selected Cooperative Games for Children and Adults.* Especially useful for teachers.

145 pp. Large format. Illustrated. Annotated bibliography. $9.95

BUILDING UNITED JUDGEMENT: A HANDBOOK FOR CONSENSUS DECISION-MAKING

Center for Conflict Resolution

Reach group unity and make your decisonmaking structure work for *you*. Maximize cooperation and fully use the creativity of all members of your group. Learn to recognize conflict as a source of growth. Handle common group problems practically.

124 pages. Large format. Illustrated. $6.95

MEETING FACILITATION: THE NO MAGIC METHOD

by Berit Lakey

Plan and carry out consistently productive meetings. Easy steps to help a group help itself.

11 pages. 50¢

DESPAIRWORK: AWAKENING TO THE PERIL AND PROMISE OF OUR TIME

by Joanna Macy

"What we urgently need is to break the taboo against expressions of despair for our world—to validate these feelings of rage and grief, realize their universality, and experience in them the mutual support that can empower us to act. To do despair-work is, in a real sense, to wake up—both to the peril and the promise."

32 pp: 1982 ISBN 0-86571-023-6 $2.45

BUILDING SOCIAL CHANGE COMMUNITIES

by the Training/Action Affinity Group

Build the social change community you need to aid you in your personal growth, social activism. How to: resolve conflicts creatively, facilitate meetings, make group decisions, form shared households, build networks for social change.

105 pages. Illustrated. ISBN 0-86571-005-8 $3.95

TWO ESSAYS: ON ANGER and NEW MEN, NEW WOMEN Some Thoughts on Nonviolence

by Barbara Deming

Thought-provoking essays adding new depth to the slogan that 'the personal is political.' Modern classics in the literature of nonviolent struggle, challenging us to recreate ourselves even as we attempt to recreate our world. Originally appeared in Barbara Deming's *We Can Not Live Without Our Lives*.

32 pp. 1982. ISBN: 0-86571-024-4 $2.45

A MANUAL FOR GROUP FACILITATORS

Center for Conflict Resolution

Get your group to work together more effectively. A working manual for learning to communicate well, doing effective planning, solving problems creatively, dealing with conflict, and moving groups toward fulfillment of their own goals.

88 pages. Large format. Illustrated. $6.00

CLEARNESS: PROCESSES FOR SUPPORTING INDIVIDUALS AND GROUPS IN DECISION-MAKING

by Peter Woodrow

Having trouble making personal decisions? Feeling isolated, alone? Don't know how to utilize other people's good thinking effectively? Handy resource for helping you think about things with the people around, develop trust, tap new resources for support, help people joining new groups. Sample agendas.

32 pp. ISBN: 0-86571-011-2 $2.45

ON ORGANIZING MACRO-ANALYSIS SEMINARS: STUDY & ACTION FOR A NEW SOCIETY

Build community even as you study your world; understand your world and *change it!* How to relate militarism to ecology, U.S. relations with the Third World to our domestic problems. Examine and develop your own visions for a better society and create informed strategies for change. Tested and used in more than 300 colleges, universities, church groups, neighborhood and community organizations.

Manual. 72 pages. Illustrated. ISBN: 0-86571-009-0 $3.95
Updated Reading List. ISBN: 0-86571-010-4 $1.75

LEADERSHIP FOR CHANGE

by Bruce Kokopeli & George Lakey

Reject authoritarian and paternalistic forms of leadership. Making practical use of feminist perspectives, break leadership functions down into their component parts to be shared and rotated, empowering all.

32 pp. Illustrated. ISBN: 0-86571-012-0 $2.45

A MODEL FOR NONVIOLENT COMMUNICATION

by Marshall Rosenberg

This groundbreaking work in interpersonal relations helps us more fully open ourselves to give and receive information, share feelings, and overcome blocks to effective communication. It is filled with illuminating examples.

40 pages. 1983. ISBN: 0-86571-029-5 $3.95

Postage and Handling: Please add $1.50 for first publication, 40¢ each additional.

Prices are subject to change • Allow 6 weeks for delivery

4722 Baltimore Ave., Philadelphia, PA 19143